Threescore And Ten: A Memorial Of The Late Albert Barnes [containing A Discourse Of That Title By Barnes, Preceded By A Memorial Sketch By D. March And Followed By Details Of The Funeral Services, And The Memorial Sermon By H. Johnson].

Albert Barnes, Daniel March

H. Adlard. Sc.

very truly yours
Albert Barnes

Threescore and Ten:

A Memorial

OF THE LATE

ALBERT BARNES.

" Mr. Barnes belonged to all Christendom. I bless God that he lived ;
I bless God that he laboured ; I thank God that he died as he died."
BISHOP STEVENS (*Protestant Episcopal Church, U.S.*).

TO THE READERS

OF

MR. BARNES'S COMMENTARIES

AND OF HIS OTHER VALUABLE WORKS,

THIS VOLUME IS DEDICATED

AS A

𝔐𝔢𝔪𝔬𝔯𝔦𝔞𝔩

OF HIS USEFUL LIFE BELOW

AND

OF HIS BLISSFUL ENTRANCE ON LIFE ABOVE.

CONTENTS.

—•◦•—

In Memoriam.

A Sketch: by the Rev. DANIEL MARCH, D.D.

PAGE

A responsible position.—Albert Barnes.—His course of study.—
Ministerial career.—A self-made man.—A worker.—His sincerity.—Candour.—Consistency.—Integrity.—Conscientiousness.
—Unboastfulness.—Kindliness.—Humility.—Earnest thought-
fulness.—Quiet trust.—Boldness of speech.—Clearness of expression.—The work of a life.—A walk by the sea-shore.—The
crystal sea above vii

—•◦•—

THREESCORE AND TEN.

A Discourse: by the late ALBERT BARNES.

The limitation of life.—Its calculableness.—Its average permanence.
—Good for the world.—Good for the individual.—The man of
seventy.—Why he should speak.—View from the summit of life.
—I. *The present.*—Life's plans ended.—Its usefulness only
incidental, rather than purposed.—Its future only beyond the
the grave.—II. *The past.*—The shaping of a man's course.—
Illustration from personal experience.—Much unrealized, which
had been planned.—A work accomplished, which had not been
anticipated.—III. Relative *value* of life in the past and present.—
Seventy years in China.—Seventy years in the dark ages.—The
last seventy years.—Progressive knowledge.—New inventions.—
Wide activities.—A fresh starting-point.—America as it was.—
America as it is.—IV. *The future.*—Hopeful prospects.—Based
on God's promises.—And on the course of events.—Universal
progressiveness.—Accumulation of forces.—No room for despondency.—Foundation of personal hopes.—A solemn choice.—
Conclusion.. 5

APPENDIX.

———

PAGE

I. THE FUNERAL SERVICES 93

II. THE ACTION OF THE CONGREGATION............................ 104

III. THE ACTION OF THE SESSION 105

IV. MEMORIAL SERMON by the Rev. Herrick Johnson, D. D.—

The orderings of Providence.—Permissive agency.—Direct
influence.—The steps of a good man.—Mr. Barnes.—Memor-
able dates.—Early scepticism.—Intellectual conviction.—
Subsequent conversion.—Ministerial studies.—Pastorate.—
The Temperance cause.—The anti-slavery question.—Bold
utterances.—Sermons at the House of Refuge.—Work as a
Commentator.—Ministerial success.—Close of life.—Last
Communion.—Last sermon.—Mental characteristics.—Balance
of mind.—Self-control.—Industry.—Method.—Firmness.—
Tenderness.—Steadfastness.—Piety.—The Master's call 107

In Memoriam.

BY THE AUTHOR OF

"NIGHT UNTO NIGHT;" "WALKS AND HOMES OF JESUS," ETC.

THE office of the sacred teacher is the highest ever held by man in this world. It is a great thing to think for one's self: it is a much greater thing to think for others. In the moments of quickened conscience it seems to us a fearful trust to be put in charge of one eternal destiny. The sacred teacher may rise to such an awful pitch of power as to form the character and fix the destiny of immortal millions. The train of thought which the sacred teacher starts may live through a whole life and overpass the boundaries of earth and time. If it be drawn from the Fountain of eternal light, it will brighten as it runs, like the rising day, and it will shine like the stars in the firmament for ever and ever. If it be drawn from the baleful fires of error, it will shed disastrous light as long.

To speak good words which shall quicken slumbering souls into spiritual life,—to expound great truths that shall gird the weak and faltering with victorious strength,—to give utterance to the cry of the poor,—to defend the cause of the oppressed,—to lift up the standard of right and liberty for the rallying of nations,—to write books over which men will bow in reverent study, as the thirsty bend to drink at living fountains,—to have one's own life and faith multiplied a millionfold in the minds of others,—to pass away from the world and leave one's work to grow with the growth of the ages, and bring forth immortal fruit long as the seasons of earth shall come and go,—such is the office of the sacred teacher whose mind God has sanctified and made strong for Himself. Such was the work, and such shall be the reward, of the honoured and beloved man whose voice has been lifted up for half a century in defence of truth and righteousness, whose name still dwells with reverence and affection upon every lip among us, and who has just passed away from the times and seasons of earth to the everlasting years of heaven.

I shall ever count it one of the rare privileges of my life that ALBERT BARNES was my personal friend, revered in my mind and beloved in my heart as few can ever be ; and now that he has passed away from the earth, and all that was mortal of him sleeps in the silent grave, I cannot refrain from attempting to tell others, who knew him less than I did, what manner of man he was to me. What I say of him shall be said, as nearly as possible, with the truthfulness and candour which were pre-eminently characteristic of the man himself. What I attempt is not eulogy, but an act of justice; not a history of his life from his youth upward, but an open, straightforward look at the man and the minister as he was in the fulness of his strength and in the maturity of age and honour.

The few facts around which gathers the fruit of his full and rounded life are soon told. He was born at Rome, in the State of New York, Dec. 1, 1798. He began life with the busiest and brightest of all the centuries, and he kept even step with the foremost in the march of the years until his journey of life was done. His first outlook upon the world found him nothing to do but to follow the trade of his father, who was a tanner. When, however, the spirit that was in him began to stir, he left the tanyard for the academy, and began the process of training for the work and warfare of intellectual life. In the hill town of Fairfield, some forty miles from his birth-place, he completed three years of college study, and then entered the Senior class at Hamilton at the age of twenty-one. His original purpose was to pursue the profession of law; but the change of the new birth came over him in the one year of his college-life, and thenceforth he left the study of the conflicting codes and statutes of time for the more profound investigation of law that is supreme and eternal. A fellow-student, with the artless simplicity of a new-born child of God, told him the story of his conversion; and that humble tale of penitence and love became the seed-corn of harvests which have already enriched the homes of millions.

Having graduated in due course at college, Mr. Barnes entered the Theological Seminary at Princeton, N. J., where he remained three years in earnest and devout preparation for the Christian ministry. At the end of one year more we find him installed as pastor of the Presbyterian church at Morristown in the same State. And then again, at the mature age of thirty-two, he assumed the responsible post, which he held for the remainder of his official life, as pastor of the First Presbyterian Church, in Philadelphia. For thirty-seven years he performed all the public duties incumbent upon his sacred office with untiring energy and with the utmost exactness and regularity. At the same time he maintained the habits of a diligent student of the Divine Word and an ardent explorer in all branches of human knowledge. He loved the walks of retirement and sacred seclusion from the selfish rivalries and the bitter contests of the world, and yet his ear was ever open to the public cry, and he was ever ready to give the support of his hand and voice to the righteous cause. He did his work with quietness and constancy, and there was little in his life to attract the applause of the world; yet a careful analysis of his character and qualities of mind will unfold excellences of the highest order, and worthy of all commendation.

In the best sense that the world ever gives to the word,

Mr. Barnes was a *self-made* man. He had indeed whatever advantage can be given by collegiate and seminary education, but he belonged to that rank of nobles in society whose title to nobility is earned by toil. And he lost none of the inherited habit of industry when he laid aside the tools of a trade to begin a life of thought. All his intellectual possessions were acquired by full and fair days' work in the field which is open to all. He took his place in the ranks of toiling men, without wealth, genius, or social distinction to give him a start; and he won success by steady, strong, two-handed conflict with all the difficulties which others have to meet. The vast results of his life-work sprang from the inspiration of industry, and the pressure of a purpose that never faltered in the face of the obstacles and discouragements which beset all human toil. He resolved to make the most and best of all the times and faculties that God had given him; and he excelled others not so much in making the resolution as in keeping it, through the toils and conflicts of a long life, to the end. There are many whose resolutions are of the best, and whose life is a continual failure. The wise and the good, the successful and the strong, are those who make fulfilment follow the right resolve as surely as the thunder-peal follows the lightning's flash.

Mr. Barnes was a most industrious and *hard-working* man; but he did not go to his toil like the galley-slave, scourged by necessity or compelled against his will. He found the joy of life in work, in the faithful use of all the faculties which God had given him, in the constant endeavour to enrich and bless the world by his toil. He loved life because it gave him opportunities to work for God and his fellow-men. He often said he would " like to live a thousand years;" and nobody who knew him thought the expression sprang from a love of ease or a desire to secure the aims of human ambition; but because he would live to witness the development of God's great providences in the progress of the world, and to bear an honourable part in the toil which shall carry light and liberty, peace and comfort, hope and salvation to all human homes. He was like one who has poured out all his treasures and efforts in laying the foundations and rearing the walls of a house for the homeless and the wretched, and he would like to live and toil on till the great house is completed and the wanderers are gathered in. He went on in his work with a steady, strong hand through all the changes of times and seasons, never bating a jot or tittle of effort from weariness, or discouragement, or opposition. The heat and the cold, the storm and the sunshine, the summer and the winter, were all alike to him seasons sent of God for the performance of life's great work. He was never withheld from the fulfilment of an appointment, by stress of weather. He could never be made to say he was tired. The busiest man in the world, he never complained that he had too much to do. He could not bear to be petted or pitied. It was in vain to offer him the easiest seat or the cosiest corner. He was bent upon making a square, bold, stand-up fight with all the burdens, toils, and hardships of human life; and he did it manfully to the end. He never learned the art of amusement : recreation for him must be another form of work. His walk in the street was the step of a man who always had something to do. For him riding on horseback was better than reclining in an easy carriage, because it was more like work. The culture of his garden with his own hands had more attraction for him than lounging at watering-places by the seaside, or reclining under the shade of trees in the cool retreats of the country. God had made him to do a man's work. He accepted the mission as prophets accepted the call of Heaven in ancient time. He bore the heat and burden of the day without complaint; and when his day closed, his work was done.

Mr. Barnes was pre-eminently an *honest* man. He was the very soul of honour in all his intercourse with his fellow-men. He never took or sought or claimed character or position or influence that was not fully and fairly his own. Of all men that I have known in a lifetime, I can think of none more manly than he. I never could see in him anything that looked like pretence or insincerity. He did not come out of himself, and lay bare the inner history of his heart for the world to read, as some men do ; but his seeming reserve did not spring from his having anything to conceal, or from fear to meet the most searching eye. His only way to gain any object was to go straightforward in open day, and let everybody see what he was seeking. The pretence, the pettiness, and the insincerity that so often mar the completeness of noble minds seemed to have no place in his. I cannot imagine the power of the temptation which would have constrained him to stoop to an act of deceit or dishonour. He loved to look at life and men and the world in the clear, steady light of truth, and it was his ruling passion to be in himself an impersonation of the truth which he loved. The look of his face, the glance of his eye, the language of his lips, the whole influence of his life as he moved among men, was a living expression of honesty, a continued homage to truth and uprightness before God and man.

In the early prime of his manhood Mr. Barnes had much to do with controversy. He was tempted as much as any man ever was to take every advantage of antagonists in debate, and to over-estimate the strength and justice of his own cause. And yet all through life he was a man of extraordinary *fairness* and *candour*. He would never resort to artifice or special pleading to gain a point. There was no trick or cunning in his mode of managing debate. His only partisanship was for the truth as it stood in his own mind, and his great aim in controversy was to set the truth in so clear a light that it could be seen in all its fulness and beauty from every point of view. I never knew a man of such strong convictions, and able to defend them so well, who was at the same time so willing to make concessions to the convictions of others. When reasoning with the sceptical and the doubting, he would put himself in their place, and give greater force to their objections and difficulties than they could themselves. He was so confident in the power of truth for its own defence that he was not afraid to set its forces upon the open field in full exposure to attack from every side. He would give the honest objector more than candour could ask : he would join hands with him in the assault, on purpose to show him that the stronghold of faith can never be stormed with double the force that sceptics can command,—that the foundations of rational and Christian belief can never be removed. He had great respect and deep sympathy for the sincere and candid doubter, and he laboured all his life long to present the claims of religion in so clear and rational a light that they must be honoured and accepted by the good sense and fair judgment of mankind. His own love of right was so intense that nothing could induce him to make light of any man's convictions, to trespass upon the freedom of any man's judgment, to intrude upon the sanctuary of any man's conscience.

He was himself thoroughly convinced that worldliness is not wisdom, either for this life or that which is to come. And when he saw men wandering away from God, and vainly endeavouring to satisfy the demands of their immortal nature by neglect of Christian duty, he pitied them for the mistake they were making. He called after them in kindliness and sympathy : "Come now, let us reason together, let us see in what direction the safe path lies." And if he could only get them to listen to his clear, earnest, candid appeal to the sense of right in their own consciences, they were sure to go away feeling that his counsel was safe and wise, even though they did not follow it. No man could give candid attention while he illustrated and enforced the claims of some great practical truth without feeling that it were better to believe as he did than the contrary—better to be such a man as he was than to be anything that he would rebuke or condemn.

Mr. Barnes was a *just* and *faithful* man in all the relations of life. Here, in this city of Philadelphia, where he lived forty years, having daily intercourse with all sorts of persons, I am confident that not one can be found who will say that Mr. Barnes ever did him wrong,—not one who will charge his memory with an act of injustice. This is a great thing to say of a man who spent much of his life in opposing opinions that were strongly cherished, and in condemning practices that were conscientiously pursued by many. It is not often that the world in the end confers the title of JUST with such unanimity upon one whose name has been a cry of resistance, or of rallying in controversy, or who has often stood in opposition to some generally accounted wise and good. It was the glory and joy of his life not only that the objects for which he contended were gained, but that the victory which he had won enriched and blessed his antagonists as much as it did himself.

He was just and faithful, both as a man and a minister. The truth that he preached to others, he practised himself. When he urged others to give in charity, he gave in like measure from his own resources. The faith, the self-denial, the integrity, which he taught from the pulpit, were best seen in his daily life by those who knew him best. He made no hasty promises. Beset, as he was, by countless applications to secure his name and to enlist his influence in behalf of private and public interests, he was careful never to awaken expectations which were not likely to be fulfilled. When he had once given his word, whether in things the least or the greatest, he never forgot—he never failed to fulfil—the engagement. Some men, who would face the tortures of the rack and the terrors of death rather than deny the faith, are careless about keeping their word in little things. Some men are pompous and particular about matters of trifling importance, and yet negligent and not to be trusted in matters of infinite moment. Mr. Barnes was just and faithful in the least and in the greatest. In the last years of his life he would go any distance, through storm and heat and cold, to fulfil an appointment, when the service rendered was entirely gratuitous, and when to most persons the stress of weather would have been sufficient reason for giving it up without question. Nothing but the arresting hand of Divine Providence could withhold him from making good his word of promise, whatever sacrifice it might cost him. And hence a few words from him of modest and measured commendation of a book, of a man, or of a cause, were generally esteemed of more value than the most extravagant testimonials from many others. His sense of truth, of justice, of integrity, was so quick and keen that no consideration of personal friendship or advantage to himself could induce him to lend his name to a dis-honourable enterprise, an untruthful representation, or an unworthy cause. No man who knew Albert Barnes as I did, could believe him capable of using artifice, intrigue, evasion, or underhand policy of any kind to gain a point. Somebody asked him in my presence if he ever went trout-fishing for recreation. "No," said he. "Why?" "Because it is all a practice of deception." He would have nothing to do with either work or amusement that depends for its interest and success upon false pretences. He was so thoroughly true and honest in his whole constitution that he would not deceive even a brute. Always generous, indulgent, easily entreated, he was intolerant only of wrong, unyield-ing and uncompromising only toward injustice and falsity.

Mr. Barnes was pre-eminently a *conscientious* man. Duty was to him a supreme law never to be superseded, never to be broken. The force and consistency, the profit and success of his laborious life, all sprang from this grandest, noblest element of character, a good conscience—a conscience void of offence toward God and toward man. He lived to do his duty, and he took thankfully the measure of happiness which must flow from such a life. Some men have a way of being conscientious, which is exceedingly troublesome to themselves and others. They are very anxious to have people know how conscientious they are. They are always telling how much it costs them. They often point to places of profit and honour that they might have held if it had not been for their consciences. They express great wonder and grief that other people's consciences are not as pure and sensitive as their own. They express the desire to do many things which they dare not because their conscience will not let them. They give the world to understand that a good conscience is a very costly thing to keep, and that, when well kept, it makes its owner quite miserable.

Mr. Barnes was not such a man. He made no boast or display of his conscientiousness. He never talked of sacrifices which he had incurred in the discharge of duty. He had so trained himself to habits of rectitude that to him the performance of duty was a second, sanctified nature. To turn out of the straight path would have given a shock to his whole constitution. To keep right on in obedience to the highest law of obligation was as much a matter of course with him as it is for the mighty river to keep its channel, or the planetary worlds to keep their orbits. There was something grand, something expressibly sublime, in the meekness and majesty, the quietness and strength, with which, in maturer life, he moved on in the undeviating track of daily duty, as if he were the most unnoticed and unknown of men, while yet he knew that millions looked to him for light on the deepest and darkest themes of human thought. He " bore his faculties so meek, he was so clear in his great office" as teacher of the word of God, that many did not see his greatness,—none but the most intimate friends knew his excellence.

With all his rigidity of virtue, his inflexible uprightness of character, his supreme devotion to truth and duty, Mr. Barnes had great *kindliness of heart*, a tender and thoughtful consideration for the feelings of others, an unfailing mindfulness of absent friends, a cordial appreciation of mementos and messages of love, a genial delight both in making and in seeing others happy. The grasp of his hand was so fervid and hearty, that few who felt it once would forget it in a lifetime. The clear, quick glance of his eye was that of a man who could look the world in the face with the openness of innocence, the courage of uprightness, and the tenderness of love. The smile of recognition, kindling upon his calm, thoughtful face, was like the breaking of the morning to men who look for the day. When he spoke a kind word of another, when he paid a pleasant compliment, when he inquired for absent friends, he did it with the simpilcity and heartiness of genuine interest. Nobody suspected him of affecting a regard which he did not feel, or of striving by any means to ingratiate himself in the good esteem of others for his own advantage. He did not make as free use of the words of compliment and courtesy as some do, but he meant and expressed more by the fewer and milder terms which he used than many do by the most extravagant professions of friendship. He never indulged in ridicule, irony, or satire, either in conversation or public address. He made no attempt at witticism or humour, but he often met his friends with a quiet and delicate playfulness of expression which in so serious and earnest a man produced all the effect of genuine humour at the moment, and passed away like the morning dew from the flowers, without leaving the stain of ridicule or the sting of satire behind.

With all his great reputation and wide-spread influence in the world, he put on no airs of importance among his brethren. He never claimed the pre-eminence, never sought to be a leader, never could be persuaded to accept the full measure of honour and deference which others desired to show him. Having the most decided opinions himself, he always paid the utmost respect to the opinions of others. He shrank from the public eye with the sensitiveness of a timid girl. I have heard him say, after forty years of preaching, he never entered the pulpit without a feeling of dread. If he had not possessed the elements of true greatness and indomitable power, his habit and strong feeling of self-depreciation would have crushed him. He never put himself on exhibition. He could not be persuaded to take a prominent seat in public meetings unless it was clearly his duty to do so. He was meek and humble, not because he had failed in life or was afraid of failure. He knew better that anybody else what grand success God had given him in his work. His excellences were not of that pitiable and negative character, which men call *goody*. He was a man of strong feeling, intense convictions, inflexible preferences, determined purpose, and yet he took a lowly place, because he kept the perfect Example ever in his eye. He walked humbly, because his walk was with God.

Mr. Barnes was a man of *faith*. With a full knowledge of the reasons which lead men to doubt, with a deep and unusual sensitiveness to the subtle suggestions of scepticism, he believed in God, in a written and inspired revelation, in the Divine character and the redeeming work of Christ, in the fitness and power of the Gospel to enlighten and save the world, in the endless retributions of joy and woe beyond the grave. Through all his working, thinking life, he stood face to face with these great facts which most deeply con-

cern man's personal duty and eternal destiny. He looked
with eager and anxious gaze upon the clouds and darkness
which are round about the Almighty, wishing that he could
more clearly see the justice and the judgments which are
the habitation of His throne. He studied the great mystery
of human life as it flows on in turbid and strong currents
through all the ages, lifting up its defiant waves against the
heaven, and peopling the infinite abyss with its crimes and
woes. He gazed with undisguised dread and horror upon
the deeper and more awful mystery of death. He could
not see, as some claim to do, smiles and roses blending on
the cold face in the coffin. He could not look down into
the grave, with the feeling that he would like to be relieved
from the toils of life, and make there his lonely bed. He
looked at all these things in their most dreadful and unques-
tionable reality. He walked solemnly round and round
upon the outermost verge of human thought and inquiry,
gazing with anxious eye into the infinite deep beyond, long-
ing to explore its mysteries and to bring back word for the
relief of troubled and doubting souls.

And yet in the face of all doubts and difficulties, he believed. He was most intelligently and profoundly a man of
faith. He had the sensibility to feel and the candour to
confess the limitations and imperfections which attend all
inquiries into the mysteries of the Divine government and
into the hidden depths of our own being and destiny. But
he had the sound judgment and the good conscience not to
throw away certainty for uncertainty. With the simplicity
of a child's faith, and with the firmness of a man's reason,
he believed the first lessons which God is teaching us now,
and he waited cheerfully and hopefully to learn more hereafter. The truth which he believed, and which he taught,
afforded him the only relief from the distress and anguish
which he would otherwise have felt in contemplating the
condition of a sinful and suffering world. He walked in

the light with a strong and joyous step, and the deepest sorrow of his life was that which weighed upon the soul of the Son of God, because men would choose darkness rather than light. I never knew a man so serious and earnest, so much in the habit of looking at the darkest side of life, who was at the same time so cheerful, so full of hope, so calm and strong in the belief that evil shall have an end and good shall triumph. If he had been a sceptic, if he had been a man of the world, if he had renounced any one of the essential principles of the Christian faith, he would have been a restless and unhappy man all his life. His earnest, truth-loving mind, his honest, practical good sense, never could have been satisfied with the sophistry of the sceptic or the sensualism of the worldling. He must rest his faith upon a strong foundation. He must have views of the Divine government and of the way of salvation, which are honourable to God and safe for man. He did so believe, and in the light and joy of that faith he lived and toiled for his fellow-men forty years, without murmuring, without despondency, without rest. He kindled the light of hope where it burns to-day in a million homes. He carried the blessing of comfort and peace to a world of sorrowing hearts. We all walk in his light; and life has been made happier and better to us all, because he lived.

Mr. Barnes was *independent* and *outspoken* on all subjects of public interest and private duty. I think he showed himself to be about the bravest and most admirable man that ever met the disturbed and misdirected currents of public opinion in his native land. Without the fiery zeal of the fanatic, without the selfish aims of the partisan, his calmness was equal to his courage, and his strength was the greater because he wasted no power in angry retort or idle declamation. He only asked that the voice of Truth might be heard, and that men would consent to abide by her instructions. He did not put himself forward as an agitator, or as the leader of a party. He only said what any just man should be willing both to hear and to say in defence of the poor and oppressed, in denunciation of vice and wrong, in commendation of liberty and order. It was inevitable that a man so upright, so honourable, so generous, so pure in heart, should many times feel himself called upon to oppose the opinions and reprove the practices of his fellow-men. And yet he did it with such deep earnestness, such calm and dispassionate reasoning, such wise and delicate consideration for the feelings of others, that he won the confidence and affection of the very men whom he rebuked. He had many conflicts to wage, but he was never a contentious man. He had no love for strife or debate. When he rebuked iniquity in his fellow-men, he was like the father who himself feels the blow with which he chastises his own child. Nothing but his own supreme love of right, of truth, of liberty, nothing but his own deep sense of obligation, could have constrained him to take up the weapons of controversy or stand forth as a reprover of the nation's sins. And if all reformers and controversialists were as wise and kind, as fair and honourable, as considerate of each other's feelings, and as willing to make concessions as he, there would be much less bitterness of strife in the world, and the cause of truth would suffer much less from its friends.

Mr. Barnes displayed the peculiar qualities of his mind most fully as an expounder of God's word. The most useful, the most widely diffused, the most generally accepted work of his life is treasured up in his twenty volumes of commentary upon different books of the Bible. The mode in which they were produced is characteristic of the man. They were all written in the early hours of the morning, before business-men have begun the day. When the lawyer appeared in his office, the merchant in his counting-room, the man of fashion at his breakfast-table, Mr. Barnes had done his day's work of authorship. In consequence of his

industrious and long-continued improvement of these early
hours, he is now, and for a long time is likely to be, the one
man to whom the greatest number of readers go to learn
what the Bible means.   Probably each Sabbath-day a million
human beings trace the lines of pages written by his hand ;
a million minds take in thought that first came from his.
Wherever the English Bible is studied, his simple, familiar,
unpretending expositions of its meaning are sure to go.
The best and truest things that are said for the instruction
of millions of Sunday-school scholars who never see his
Notes, come from him.   It often seems to me as if there
were something unspeakably awful in the responsibility
resting upon the one man from whom so many derive their
impressions of the meaning and value of the Word of life.
And yet God clothed his servant with humility, that he
might not lead his fellow-men astray.   God gave him great
clearness and simplicity of character, that he might guide
others more safely in the path of life.   God made him meek
and just, devout and prayerful, that he might more easily
learn the mind of the Spirit, and so teach others with such
simplicity as that with which children must be taught.

His clear, strong, honest, practical good sense is the
secret of his power and the source of his success in ex-
pounding God's Word.   Others have displayed more learning than he ;—Mr. Barnes surpasses all others in that good
sense which everybody understands, in that simplicity which
the common people love, in that fulness and fidelity which
is adapted to all capacities, in that fairness and candour
which disarms opposition, and in that fervent and practical
aim which reaches every heart.   Some think he says the
same thing too many times over.   He knew well that repe-
tition is the secret of success in teaching.   Truth once
spoken is seldom understood, more seldom believed.   Some
think him not profound because he is always clear.   They
forget that muddy waters are not necessarily deep.   Mr.

Barnes makes dark things so plain that his readers sometimes forget that they ever were dark.   He faces difficulties so calmly, and overcomes them with so little parade of strength, that many think a common man might do the same thing.

But this man whom we all knew so well, who moved among us with so much meekness and gentleness, who worked for the good of others so faithfully for forty years, was no common man.   There has been no other like him in all our American history.   I look the world over in vain to find his equal in the rare combination of meekness and courage, quietness and strength, modesty and worth, self-command and self-control, friendship for man and devotion to God, simplicity of private life and power over millions to teach them the word of truth.   He has passed away in the glory of his great manhood, in the eternal prime of virtue, faith, and Christian honour.   Already his noble life-work has made him a name and a praise unto the ends of the earth ; and in the glorious kingdom of the ransomed above, there shall be multitudes from many nations to call him blessed, there shall be millions to testify their gratitude for the guidance which he gave them in the way of life.

A few summers ago, Mr. Barnes, as his custom was, went down to the seaside to gather new vigour from the strength of the deep for his autumn work.   While there, he was walking alone along the sandy beach, hearing in the music of the waves the solemn murmur of that sea which we must all sail so soon, when a stranger met him with an earnest and searching look, and then passed on.   A few moments afterward the stranger met one who knew him, and learned by inquiry that the person whose striking figure had arrested his attention was the one man in all the world who has taught the greatest number of readers to understand and to love the word of God.   He returned to Mr. Barnes, and with great courtesy and dignified propriety of address, begged to be permitted to tell him how much his mind had been enlightened, his faith strengthened, and his heart comforted, by studying the "Notes on the New Testament." That stranger was a native of another country, a gentleman of culture and high position in his own land, and he thought it a memorable day in his life when he met Mr. Barnes on the beach, and told him how much he honoured his name and prized his work.

And so now I love to think of Albert Barnes as walking on the shore of the crystal sea of heaven, his face radiant with a light that never shone on earthly sea or shore, and there—not one, but—thousands from many lands, meeting him with joy, and telling him how much he had enriched them by his life of toil, and how much it makes heaven seem like home to find him there; and I love to think of him there in the same modest and manly spirit which marked his character here, ascribing the glory of all he did unto Him that sitteth upon the throne, and unto the Lamb for ever and ever.

DANIEL MARCH.

Philadelphia, 1871.

THREESCORE AND TEN.*

—◆◆◆—

" The days of our years are threescore years and ten."

Ps. xc. 10.

—◆◆◆—

ALL earthly life, so far as we have an opportunity of observing it, has an outer limit: a boundary which cannot be passed. Death reigns, and apparently has always reigned, in our world; for there is not now in the air, on the earth, or in the waters, a living thing that existed at the creation.

This limitation in regard to life is by no means the same in all orders of beings. Each class of animals, of birds, of fishes, is subject to its own law in this respect, as if it were entirely independent of all other beings,—and has a limitation of its own. Life may be almost momentary in one class, as in the

* The substance of the following discourse was delivered in the First Presbyterian Church, Philadelphia, December 6th, 1868, just two years before the time of the author's lamented decease, December 24th, 1870.

insect that sports in the summer sun for an hour, and then dies; it may extend, as in the old trees that stand on the African or Pacific coast, for many thousands of years. But still, there is a boundary which is not to be passed. It is not the same in the horse, in the eagle, in the elephant, in the gazelle, in the humming-bird, in the whale, and in man—in the oak of Bashan, in the cedar of Lebanon, and in the hyssop that springs out of the wall—for each and all of these have their separate laws of limitation, and that which belongs to one cannot be transferred to another. A boundary has been fixed, in each and every case, beyond which no vigour of frame, no tenacity of life, no devices for restoring the wastes in the animal economy, and no remedial or recuperative arrangements can carry any one. Time does not modify this law. Improvements and remedies in other things do not affect it, or produce any change. The age of the horse, the oak, and the lion, is the same as it was in the days of Abraham, and, so far as appears, will remain the same to the end of time. So fixed is this law that it clearly proves that over all this there is a Presiding Mind; that the arrangement is the result of the will of the Great Ruler of the world.

Yet though the period of life in different orders of beings is so varied, it is in each particular and separate order so regular, that it can be made the subject of most accurate calculation, and can be laid at the foundation of some of the most important arrangements in society. At the foundation of all this there is an important general law, the knowledge of which is now exerting an important influence on the affairs of men,—a law, the reason of which no one can explain, but he who believes in the existence and the superintending providence of God. It is now established as certain, that of a given number of persons, almost precisely the same number will die in each year at the same period of life, and even ordinarily by the same forms of disease. In like manner, it has become the subject of most accurate computation that almost precisely the same losses of property will occur by sea or on land—by fire or by shipwreck—so that the regularity of such losses can be made the basis of most important pecuniary calculations and responsibilities. This science, comparatively new, is the foundation of all the arrangements in annuity companies, in marine, fire, and life insurance companies, the operations of which are founded on calculations made on the average continuance of human life, and on the probability that any given number of casualties will occur, or that any given number of persons will die at any one period of life in any single year. So accurate is this science that no investments are more safe than those which are based on such calculations, and that there is no class of pecuniary institutions more certainly destined to become universal. The world is not governed by chance, but by certain laws; and the result of the operations of insurance companies will tend, like our study of the physical laws of nature, to confirm men more and more in the belief that there is a God, and that the world is governed by regular laws.

In man the usual limit of life is "threescore years and ten." By this it is not meant, of course, that no one ever passes over that line; but that this is the ordinary and common period, beyond which man does not pass—as there is an ordinary and fixed limit in the age of the horse, the lion, the eagle, the humming-bird, the honey-bee. There are exceptions to most general laws, but there are no more in regard to the life of man than in other things.

It is remarkable that this was the allotted period in the time of Moses, (if the Psalm from which the motto is taken was written by him, as it purports to have been,) and that the law has remained unchanged to the present time—just as the law in regard to the duration of life has remained the same in regard to the inhabitants of the air, the earth, and the waters. The life of the lion or the eagle has neither been lengthened nor abridged during that period; nor have these long centuries done anything to extend or diminish the length of life anywhere in the animal or vegetable creation.

This fact is especially remarkable in man, because the highest talent has been exerted to find out some method to lengthen his existence on the earth. One profession, found in all countries, embracing in its ranks those who have been among the most eminent in learning and skill, has been especially devoted to the inquiry whether the ordinary causes which abridge human life could not be modified or removed, and whether there could not be found in nature some hidden power—some "Elixir of Life"—by which the days of man might be multiplied upon the earth. Yet all in vain. No secret in nature has been discovered to check the ravages of death, and to make man immortal; and it is equally true that no secret has been discovered by which the settled law in regard to the general limit of life can be changed, or by which men can be carried far beyond the period of "threescore and ten." In nothing has science been more baffled and rebuked than in this; and, much as it has done to remove disease, to alleviate suffering, to administer comfort to the dying, or to increase (perhaps) the *average* length of life, it has done absolutely nothing to change the fixed boundary of human existence, nor is there now the slightest probability that it will do it in the time to come.

The tables by which the calculations in life annuities and insurances are now regulated, and which are so accurate, will be as certain a basis for such calculations in coming ages, and those tables will continue to mock, as they do now, all the boasted achievements and promises of science.

In regard to *man*, and especially to man considered as a fallen and sinful being, and with reference to the problem of redemption, many reasons might be suggested why the usual limit of his probation should have been fixed at "threescore years and ten."

The *great purposes to be accomplished in the world can be thus better secured* than they could be by one which would greatly protract the life of man. The present arrangement has all the advantage of bringing varied powers upon the earth to meet the new circumstances of the world in the development of the Divine plans;—the advantage, perhaps, of bringing more actors on the stage, and of preparing more immortal beings for a future world;—the advantage of greatly multiplying the number of the redeemed, and consequently of glorifying the Redeemer and augmenting the joys of heaven;—the advantage of preventing the evils which would arise from a vast accumulation of wealth and power in the hands of a few individuals, and the creation of a permanent tyranny in the hands of a few men. It is far better for the liberty and happiness of the mass of men that a man of accumulated or accumulating wealth should lose his hold on his property at the age of "threescore and ten," and that it should be distributed in society, than that he should be allowed to go on absorbing the wealth of the world for a thousand years,—as it was of advantage to the world that Xerxes, Cæsar, Alexander, and Napoleon should die, rather than that they should live to confirm and establish a tyranny for centuries. It is an advantage to the world that men should die ; that, having accomplished their great purpose of life, they should give place to others ; and that what they have gained in any respect should go into the common stock for the good of the world at large, and for the benefit of coming generations, rather than that it should be retained by themselves under the form of vast monopolies.

At the same time it is to be remarked that a man will be *more likely to attend to the interests of his soul* when he knows that the affairs of the world are of so little importance to him, and that all that he can acquire must soon—very soon—pass into other hands, than he would if he felt that what he could gain would continue to be his, and would be constantly increasing for a thousand years. As man, therefore, is a fallen being ;—as his great interests lie, beyond the grave ;—as this is essentially a world of probation;—as all that any one can gain here is a trifle of no value compared with the great interests beyond the tomb;—as it is desirable that he should constantly feel and realize this;—as it is important that all the means possible should be used to fix his attention on these facts, and to prevent his jeoparding his eternal interests by neglect and delay,—and as the period of seventy years furnishes ample time to prepare for the world beyond, and to secure the salvation of the soul, we can see that it is a wise and benevolent arrangement by which this should be the general limit of human life. Man must be content with this. He has no power to remove the limit. Science, time, experience, prudence, medicines, do nothing to modify this law of our being, or to secure to us any longer duration on earth than God has assigned us.

If an apology were demanded of one who has reached the period of threescore and ten, for his presuming to refer to himself and to his views of life, it might be found, perhaps, in the following considerations :

1. That though, in the aggregate, the number of men who reach that period of life is not small, yet almost none give utterance in any public or permanent form to their own views and impressions in regard to that period of life, or to the results of their

own observation and experience in reference to human affairs, in church or state, during the time through which they have lived.

2. That the young, for the most part, hope to reach that period; and it may be presumed to be a matter not without interest to them, to know how life will seem to them *when* they reach it. It may be supposed to be useful to them, in forming their own plans, to place themselves, as far as possible, *in* that position, and from that "standpoint" to inquire what is worth living for and what not; what will then commend itself to them as wise and good, and what not; what the world is in reality, as compared with what it seems to be when the colourings of a youthful imagination are thrown over it in anticipation. Every young man has a right to catechise an aged man as to what life is, and what the world is.

3. There is often an impression that old men take a gloomy view of life: that the result of their experience is merely disappointment; that all which they have to say is that the visions of early years have vanished, leaving nothing substantial or worth living for; that the world to them is gloomy, and that the effect of their experience has been to make them sullen, sour, and morose; that they see only decay and ruin around them; that as age comes upon

them, they see in religion only corruption of doctrine, in morals only degeneracy, in political affairs only a weakening of the powers of just government, in the boasted advances of science only that which tends to sap the foundation of true religion, and which threatens the overthrow of all that hitherto has commanded the assent of the wisest and the best of the race, and which is essential to the well-being of society.

4. Every man who has reached that period of life *ought* to be able to say something which will be useful to those who are forming their plans, and who are looking out on the great world as the theatre of future action. He has indeed lived in vain who has passed so many years upon the earth if he has gained *nothing* that may be of use as counsel to those who are to come after him;—who has laid up nothing that will add to the common stock of human knowledge, or contribute to human improvement and to the progress of the world.

5. As a further apology for speaking in the manner in which I propose to do, it may be added that most of the things which I shall say might be spoken by one man as well as another, at my time of life. It is the mere fact that one *has* reached that period which entitles him to the privilege of speaking to a coming generation, or of giving utterance to the results of

his observation and experience, and not anything which has been peculiar in his own history, or because he has any special claim to be heard by the world. There was force as well as obvious fitness in what the young man Elihu, as recorded in the book of Job, said, "Days should speak, and multitude of years should teach wisdom," Job xxxii. 7. It is a common feeling among men that those who are about to leave the world should be allowed to speak, and that a respectful attention should be given to their utterances, whether those utterances are on the calm bed of death, or are the language of the martyr at the stake; whether they are the utterances of age, or of the criminal about to meet the just sentence of the law. For myself, what I shall say, if I shall say anything that will be worthy of attention, will be derived mostly from the mere fact that the seventy years which have thus been travelled over are among the most eventful that have occurred in the history of the world, and that those years themselves utter most solemn counsels to those who are to fill up the next seventy years of the world's history.

He who has reached this period must regard himself as now entering on the last stage of his existence on earth. He has reached the summit of life. He cannot expect or hope to rise higher. He has come to the top of the hill, and must soon pass over to the other side. He may find there—or may think he has found, as one sometimes does when he ascends a mountain—a little spot which seems to be level ground—a small area of table-land—a plateau—that spreads out a little distance around him. If he is permitted to walk for a few years on that plateau—that table-land—that level spot,—it is all that he can now hope for. He can look for no greater degree of vigour of body or of mind; for no greater ability to labour. That little spot of level ground which he seems to have found on the summit, spreads out before him with much that is inviting. He could not deny that he would, on many accounts, love to linger there, and extend his walk farther than he can reasonably hope that he will be permitted to do. He cannot conceal it from himself that though this little spot *seems* to be level, yet that it will soon begin to slope in the other direction, or that he may soon come to a precipice down which he may suddenly fall, to rise no more. The ascent to that little level or plateau was gradual and long. While ascending, it was uncertain whether the summit would ever be reached at all, and what it would be found to be should it be reached: whether it would be found covered with clouds and agitated with storms, or whether it would be serene and calm and clothed with sunshine.

So one ascends a lofty mountain. The summit lies in the distance, now with bright sunshine settling on it, and now covered and obscured by clouds, and wholly shut out from view. In the ascent, as he passes from one eminence to another, now he enjoys a wide and varied and beautiful prospect; now he "fears as he enters into a cloud;" now the cloud lifts itself, and discloses a prospect of distant woods and fields and rivers and villages and farmhouses, so varied and so beautiful as to reward him for all his toil thus far; and now a cloud settles again on his path, and the ascent becomes more difficult, more rocky, more steep; and then the cloud breaks away and the summit shows itself near, and his steps are lighter and his heart is more buoyant, as if all the difficulties were soon to be overcome. The summit is at last reached. It may be a sharp point of rock; it may be utterly barren; it may be covered with perpetual snow; it may be enveloped in clouds, and there may be a raging storm of hail and sleet; it may be a place so cold, so dreary, so barren, that he at once turns his footsteps and hastens down the path that he trod in the ascent. Or he may find there a level plain; he may have a glorious sunshine; he may have wide and beautiful prospects—distant hills and valleys, streams and lakes and waterfalls, towns and villages and cultivated farms all around him, and the blue ocean in the distance, and he may linger there, and wish that he could tarry longer—fully rewarded for all his toil and fatigue. The ascent was long and slow and gradual. The descent must be precipitous, quick, sudden. The termination is not far off—*the grave.*

Of one arrived at advanced years, a young man would have the right to ask, "How does life *seem* now? And how ought such views as one takes at the age of threescore-and-ten to influence those who are just entering on their course, in regard to their own views, plans, and purposes? In what way should a young man form his plans if he would make that experience his own? In what way would a man who *has* reached that period form his plans of living, if he could now begin life anew?"

I will tell you, in as few words as possible, how I feel at this period of life. What I shall say, I trust, will not make you gloomy, or dispirited, or sad. It will not lead you to think that there is nothing worth living for, though I would hope that it might lead those who are setting out on life to modify their plans by a contemplation of the feelings and views which will come over their own minds when the plans of life are about to close.

I.

THE first thought is, that *one who has reached this period has come to an end of all his plans, arrangements, and purposes,* in regard to this world. The schemes of life, whatever they may have been, are ended. This is to him a new thought—a thought which he has never experienced before, and of which he has not been before in a situation to form a conception: and this thought I would be glad to impress on the minds of those who are younger,—that the time must soon come when all their earthly plans must be ended; when there will be no new schemes for them to form, no new purposes of life to execute.

It is, and must be, difficult for those who are yet in the vigour of life to form a conception of the state of mind when this becomes a reality; when a man feels, as he has never felt before, that there is little more for him to do. But though it may be difficult to form a conception of a condition so different from what he has as yet experienced, it may not be unprofitable to advert for a moment to the fact, and to state, as clearly as possible, what the feeling is when this conviction first comes over the mind.

A man rarely forms any new plans of life at seventy years of age. He enters no new profession or calling, he embarks in no new business, he undertakes to write no new book, he forms no new friendships, alliances, or partnerships; he cannot feel, as he once could, that on the failure of one plan he may now embark in another with better promise of success.

Hitherto, all along his course of life he has felt that, if he became conscious of having mistaken his calling, or if he was unsuccessful in that calling, he might embrace another; if he was disappointed or failed in one line of business, he might resume that line, or embark in another with energy and hope; for he had youth on his side, and he had (or thought he had), many years before him. If one friend proved unfaithful, he might form other friendships. If he failed in his chosen profession, the world was still before him where to choose, and there were still many paths that might lead to affluence or to renown. If he lost one battle, the case was not hopeless, for he might yet be honoured on some other field with victory, and be crowned with glory.

But usually, when a man reaches the period of " threescore and ten years," all these things lie in the past. His purposes have all been formed and ended.

If he sees new plans and purposes that seem to him to be desirable or important to be executed, if there are new fields of honour, wealth, science, ambition, or benevolence,—they are not for him, they are for a younger and a more vigorous generation. It is true that this feeling *may* come over a man at any period of life. In the midst of his way, in the successful prosecution of the most brilliant purposes, in the glow and ardour attending the most attractive schemes, the hand of disease or of death may be laid on him, and he may be made to feel that all *his* plans are ended—a thought all the more difficult to bear because he has not been prepared for it by the gradual whitening of his hairs and the infirmities of age.

Hezekiah, king of Israel, expressed the feelings of such a man, when, in the vigour of his years and in the midst of his schemes, he was suddenly smitten by disease, and brought apparently near the grave. " I said in the cutting off of my days, I shall go to the gates of the grave : I am deprived of the residue of my years. Mine age is departed, and is removed from me as a shepherd's tent : I have cut off like a weaver my life : he will cut me off with pining sickness : from day even to night wilt thou make an end of me. The grave cannot praise thee ; death cannot celebrate thee : they that go down into the pit cannot hope for thy truth " (Isa. xxxviii. 10—18).

C

A few remarks may illustrate this point.

(1.) It was a great problem so to frame the world, and so to endow man, as to secure the activity of the race; and there are two great laws by which that activity is secured. The one is, that in each and every generation there is enough for all men *to do;* the other is, that there is at any time talent enough to accomplish all that is *needful to be done.* In the numerous and various professions and callings of life, —in agriculture, commerce, the mechanic arts, the fine arts,—in the pursuits of literature and science,— in the education of the young,—in the necessary attendance on the sick, and the care of the infirm and the helpless,—in extracting ores and the precious metals from the earth,—in levelling forests, and in making roads, bridges, and canals,—in the works of architecture, ship-building, and machines for labour, —in navigating rivers and oceans,—there is always *enough* for any one generation to do: so much to do, that none need be unemployed or idle.

At the same time, there is always talent enough on the earth to accomplish what is needful to be done. If, in addition to the usual employments of mankind, any great emergency arises,—if society has reached a point where it is to be raised to a higher level, and the ordinary measures of human endowment are not equal to the emergency, higher talent adapted to the emergency is brought upon the stage, and the affairs of the world are raised *to* that higher level, and move forward *on* that higher level till another similar emergency arises. Columbus, Galvani, Galileo, Newton, Watt, Fulton, Morse, appear at the proper time; for God creates great intellects when He pleases, and brings them upon the world to carry out His own great plans, when the world is ripe for them. No enterprise fails for want of talent; no created talent need be idle for want of employment.

(2.) Within a limited range men are so endowed that they may succeed perhaps almost equally well in one, or two, or three, or four professions or callings.* It is implied in this statement that that range is not large. A man may be a farmer, *or* a mechanic, *or* a merchant, *or* a sailor, and possibly he might succeed in either of these vocations. He may, therefore, make his choice between them, or may, to a limited extent, change from one to another; that is, if unsuccessful in one, he may find success in another, or if any particular emergency in the world's affairs shall make an additional number necessary in one occupa-

---

* This was true of Michael Angelo. On his tomb, in the church of Santa Croce, in Florence, are inscribed the words :

> " Michaeli Angelo Bonarotio,
> E vetusta Simoniorum familiâ,
> *Sculptori, Pictori, et Architecto,*
> Famâ omnibus notissimo."

tion, that emergency may be met by this adaptedness to different employments—this *play*, or room for free action, in the wheels by which the affairs of the world are moved.

But no one can succeed equally well in all the employments of life. A man must, as a general law, be a farmer, *or* a mechanic, *or* a merchant, *or* a sailor, *or* a professional man; he must be either a lawyer, *or* a physician, *or* a clergyman; he must be either a poet, *or* an orator, *or* a man of science—he cannot be all. There have been a few men of so diversified talent that they have secured, in each of three or four departments of science, what would have made them eminent if they had been equally distinguished in any one department; such men have been rare in the world.

It was necessary, in order to secure the accomplishment of the great purposes of society, that there should be this *play* in the endowments of man; that it should be so arranged that success might be secured in any one employment within this limited range; that there might be, to a certain extent, room for a choice in a profession; that there might be enough talent upon the earth at any one time to accomplish all the purposes of society, and that it might be certain that all these various callings and professions would be filled.

(3.) It is further to be remarked, that men are so endowed with propensities towards a particular calling, or with such an inclination towards a particular calling, as to make it certain that what is necessary to be done *will* be done. This great matter has not been left to chance. God designed that all these professions and callings should be filled, and hence he made it certain in the very constitution of men, and in the arrangements of society, that that purpose should be accomplished. Hence it is that there are always those who are willing to cultivate the earth; to engage in the mechanic arts; to navigate rivers, lakes, and oceans; to dig canals; to explore unknown regions; to be the pioneers in extending the limits of civilization; to perform surgical operations; to attend in the hospitals for the blind, the dumb, the insane; to minister to the wants of the sick and the dying; nay, to engage in the most humble and menial employments. No profession or calling languishes because there are none who are willing to engage in it; no interest of society suffers because it is too laborious, or too perilous, or too humble, or too painful to be performed.

As an illustration of this thought, I may refer to the necessity that there should be *sailors* in the world. There are few parents, if any, who would desire that their sons should be seamen; there are

few who in fact do not oppose it when their sons
manifest a preference for the occupation of a sailor.
Yet the navigation of the ocean, the intercourse of
nations by sea, the pursuits of commerce, are indis-
pensable for the advancement of the race and the
good of mankind. God designs that there shall be,
in every age, persons in large number who will be
willing to spend their lives on the ocean, and hence
there is among the young, in each generation, a
sufficient number who manifest an early propensity
for the life of a sailor; and hence, too, when this idea
takes possession of the mind of a boy, nothing will
ordinarily turn him from his purpose. No promise
of ease or comfort or a more lucrative business on
land, no attractions of home, no love of friends, no
prospect of honour or of affluence in another calling
will turn him from his purpose, or drive the thought
from his mind. God thus, in the furtherance of His
own purposes, secures what could not otherwise be
secured, by laying this purpose and this desire in the
minds of as many of each generation as are necessary
to navigate the seas and to keep up the commerce of
the world.

(4.) In accordance with these principles, a man
may, within a very limited range, make a change in
his profession. If he is unsuccessful in that calling
which he has chosen,—if he finds that the profession

is already full,—if he discovers that he is not fitted for it, and is not able to succeed in it,—he may, in early life and within a limited range, exchange it for another, and within that range may find a door of usefulness or of honour still open to him. The young farmer may become a merchant or a student; he who has been trained to the mechanic arts may become a member of one of the learned professions; or he who has been destined by his early circumstances, or by parental purpose, to an humble occupation, may rise to the higher walks of life, and make his name known abroad in his own or in foreign lands. But no man can safely venture often on such a change. One such change may peril nothing; perhaps a second would not endanger the great ends of life; but beyond this no man is safe. Life is too short to make many experiments of this kind; and beyond what has now been suggested, life would become vacillating, and would pass away with no fixed purpose, and in the end man would have accomplished nothing.

(5.) To him, however, who has reached the period of threescore and ten years, no such change is usually possible; no such new plan to be entered on. The purpose of life is accomplished; the changes have been all passed through. There is no new profession to be chosen; there are no new plans to be formed; there is no new distinction to be acquired; there are no books to be written, no houses to be built, no fields to be cultivated, no forests to be levelled, no works of art that are to be entered on. Painful as the thought may be, the business walks of life have no place for the aged man; there is no place for him in the social circles of the gay, in the mercantile calling, at the bar, in the medical profession, in the pulpit, on the bench, in the senate-chamber, in embassies to foreign courts. Distinction and honours are no longer to be divided between him and his competitors; and the accumulating wealth of the world is no more to be the subject of partnership between him and others. Without plan, now, except as to the future world,—his old companions, rivals, and friends having fallen by the way,—the active pursuits of life and the offices of trust and honour now in other hands,—the busy world not caring for his aid, and hoping nothing from him, it is his now (except so far as the friends of earlier years may have been spared to him,—or as he may have secured the respect of the new generation that is coming on the stage of action,—or as he may do good by matured wisdom in counsel, or by the distribution of wealth accumulated in other years, or by an example of gentleness, meekness, and patience amid the infirmities of age, illustrating the influence of religion and the blessedness of hope as he walks tremblingly on the verge of the tomb) to tread his solitary way, already more than half forgotten, to the grave. He has had his day, and the world has nothing more to give him or to expect from him.

Most men in active life look forward, with fond anticipation, to a time when the cares of life will be over, and when they will be released from its responsibilities and burdens; if not with an absolute desire that such a time should come, yet with a feeling that it will be a relief when it does come. Many an hour of anxiety in the counting-room, many an hour of toil in the workshop or on the farm, many an hour of weariness on the bench, many a burdened hour in the great offices of state, and many an hour of exhaustion and solicitude in professional life, is thus relieved by the prospect of rest—of absolute rest—of entire freedom from responsibility. What merchant and professional man, what statesman, does not look forward to such a time of repose, and anticipate a season—perhaps a long one—of calm tranquillity before life shall end? And when the time approaches, though the hope often proves fallacious, yet its approach is not unwelcome. Diocletian and Charles V. descended from their thrones to seek repose, the one in private life, the other in a cloister; and the aged judge, merchant, or pastor, welcomes

the time when he feels that the burden which he has
long borne may be committed to younger men.

Yet when the time of absolute rest comes, it is
different from what had been anticipated. There is,
to the surprise, perhaps, of all such men, this new,
this strange idea,—an idea which they never had
before, and which did not enter their anticipations,—
that they have now nothing to live for; that they have
no motive for effort; that they have no plan or purpose
of life. They seem now to themselves, perhaps to
others, to have no place in the world; no right in it.
Society has no place for them, for it has nothing to
confer on them, and they can no longer make a place
for themselves. General Washington, when the war
of Independence was over, and he had returned to
Mount Vernon, is said to have felt "lost," because he
had not an army to provide for daily; and Charles V.,
so far from finding rest in his cloister, amused himself,
as has been commonly supposed, in trying to make
clocks and watches run together, and so far from actually withdrawing from the affairs of state—miserable in
his chosen place of retreat—still busied himself with
the affairs of Europe, and sought in the convent at
Yuste to govern his hereditary dominions which he
had professedly resigned to his son, and as far as
possible still to control the empire where he had so
long reigned. The retired merchant, unused to

reading, and unaccustomed to agriculture or the mechanical arts, having little taste, it may be, for the fine arts or for social life, finds life a burden, and sighs for his old employments and associations ; for as he has professedly done with the world, so the world has actually done with him.

How great, therefore, is the difference in the condition of a man of twenty and one of seventy years ! To those in the former condition, the words of Milton in relation to our first parents, when they went out from Eden into the wide world, may not improperly be applied—

> " The world was all before them where to choose
> Their place of rest, and Providence their guide ;"—

those in the other case have nothing which they can choose. There is nothing before them but the one path—that which leads to the grave—to another world. To them the path of wealth, of fame, of learning, of ambition, is closed for ever.

I do not mean to say that there *can* be nothing for an aged man to do, or that there *may* not be, in some cases, a field of usefulness—perhaps a new and a large one—for him to occupy. I mean only, that this cannot constitute a part of his *plan* of life ; it cannot be the result of a purpose formed in his earlier years. His own plans and purposes of life are ended ; and whatever there may be in reserve for

him, it is usually a new field—something which
awaits him beyond the ordinary course of events;
and the transition from his own finished plans to
this cannot but be deeply affecting to his own mind.
I do not affirm that a man may not be useful and
happy as long as God shall lengthen out his days on
the earth; and I do not deny that there may be
much in the character and services of an aged man
that should command the respect and secure the
gratitude of mankind. The earlier character and the
earlier plans of every man should be such that he
will be useful if his days extend beyond the ordinary
period allotted to our earthly life. A calm, serene,
cheerful old age is always useful. Consistent and
mature piety, gentleness of spirit, kindness and
benevolence are always useful. It is useful to the
advancing generation, to show that, even amid the
infirmities of age, there is enough to make a man
calm, cheerful, happy; that age is not necessarily
morose or misanthropic; that though a man has
practically done with the more active enterprises of
life, he does not cease to feel an interest in what
occupies the attention of those who bear the heat
and the burdens of the day, or even in the innocent
amusements and pastimes of childhood and youth.
It does good, moreover, to the advancing generation
to afford them an opportunity of developing their own

character, and manifesting their own kindness by
showing proper respect for age, and by thus cheering
those who are descending into the valley of years.
By his mature counsels also, by his practical wisdom,
by the results of his long observation and experience,
an aged man may do much to promote the welfare
of the world; and it may be a calamity that will be
deeply felt by survivors, long after his own plans of
life shall have been ended, when he is gathered to
his fathers. If he cannot now form new plans to be
executed by himself, he may infuse the results of his
own long experience and observation into the schemes
formed by those in the vigour of life,—thus com-
bining the wisdom of years with the ardour of youth.
He may be the patron of learning, of science, of the
useful or the ornamental arts: he may mingle with
others in the works of Christian charity; he may
do good by showing to the coming generation that
there is, in his apprehension, much that is worth
living for in this world, and much to hope for in the
world to come. Or, perchance, there *may be* open
before him in old age some new field of usefulness,
unthought of in earlier life, that never entered into
his own designs, but which may, after all, be that for
which he will be gratefully remembered, and which
will perpetuate his influence on the earth; some field
of charity to cultivate, some work of benevolence to

perform, for which he has been spared to the world beyond the ordinary period allotted to man.*

If an inference should be drawn from the above remarks, it should not be one of despondency and gloom. There are cheerful views which an aged man may take of life, perhaps not less cheerful than those which are taken in early years. If early life is full of hope, it is also often full of anxiety and un-

---

* As an illustration of this last remark, it cannot be improper to refer to the case of one, a most venerable man, not long since removed from the world, John Adams, LL.D., for many years the well-known principal of Phillips Academy, Andover, Mass. His name is widely known and honoured by those who enjoyed the benefit of his instructions. By his talents and learning and fidelity he made that institution what it was, and gave it the first place among the classical schools of the land.

He accomplished the work which he had contemplated, and then, after many years' service, carried out another plan which he had long cherished, of "retiring" from the post when he should have reached the ordinary term allotted to human life. He therefore resigned his position, and removed to what was then the new state of Illinois. Finding himself in robust health, unwilling—perhaps it might be said *unable*—to spend his time without some useful occupation, he employed himself, at first as a recreation, in the establishment of Sabbath-schools. In this benevolent work he traversed the state, founded large numbers of Sabbath-schools, put the system on a permanent foundation during the period of nearly twenty years, and then, at the age of *ninety-one,* closed the *second* work of his life, venerated and esteemed by all. As the result of these mature labours, it is supposed that there are not less than fifty thousand children regularly in the Sabbath-schools in the state of Illinois, who would not have been there if it had not been for services he rendered to the church and the world *beyond* the period of "threescore and ten."

certainty; if in advanced life the world has now nothing to offer to a man, it may be that much is gained by being free from the cares, the burdens, and the anxieties of earlier years; if to such a one this world has nothing now to give, there may be much more than it ever gave even in anticipation, and infinitely more than it has given in reality, in the hope of the life to come—in the prospective happiness of heaven now so near.

But lessons of another kind may be drawn from this view, that may be valuable to those who are entering on life. They are such as the following:

They who are in early or in middle life should not look for happiness in that future period when they shall be laid aside by age, and prevented from engaging in the active duties and responsibilities of life. True happiness is found in useful employment; in doing our duty; in improving the present—not in dreams and visions of the future. The young and the vigorous should make the most of the present. The present is all that they can calculate on with any certainty, or with any such probability as to be the foundation of a plan of living. They who are anticipating happiness in the distant future on earth—when they shall reach old age—may not, probably will not, reach that period; and they may be much disappointed in their anticipations if they do.

The plans of this life should extend as far into the future as possible; so far, that if it can be done, they should embrace the whole of life: in other words, so that the time will never come when they shall feel that they have *nothing to do.*

All classes of men should so live that when the period of old age shall arrive, if they reach that period, they may be able to look back on a life well spent—not with the embittered feelings that their lives have been wasted; not with the painful reflection, when they can form *no* plan of life, that the time when they *could* have formed a purpose that might have extended far into the future, and that might have benefited the world, was squandered and lost.

I may add also, that that man is indeed desolate who has reached the period of "threescore and ten" with no hope of a future life; with no evidence that he is prepared for heaven; with nothing to anticipate in a coming world. I shall not be understood as intimating that I regard religion as not valuable or necessary at any period of life: but in its earlier periods there *are* other things which may engage the attention; there are other hopes which may be before the mind; the world, then, has much to promise, if not much to give; there are plans that may be formed that will engross the attention, hopes that may fill the mind with ardour, prizes to be won which seem to be worth all the efforts which they will cost. What is there of this nature for the aged man at the close of life? What plan, what hope can he now have, if it is not derived from religion? What is there for him to live for, if it is not the life to come? What a blank *must* existence now be to him, if he has no prospect of life and joy beyond the grave!

II.

TANDING at this point of life, all men could see, if they would reflect, *that there has been a higher plan or purpose, even in their own affairs, than their own; and that there has been an influence continually bearing on themselves to carry out that higher plan.* In other words, a man will often see that he has not accomplished what he designed to do, but perhaps the very reverse, in the execution of some higher purpose than his own.

If such reflections should lead one to recognize an overruling hand in his own life, and if it should lead to the conviction that there is a great comprehensive plan which embraces all human affairs, and which makes all the individual purposes of men subordinate to that, it would be a result that might do much to enable him to form a just estimate of the real course of things. That there *is* a vast and comprehensive purpose, so to speak, *above us*—a purpose that embraces all our individual actions, and all the affairs of nations, making all tributary to the accomplishment of a high and eternal plan—as each fountain of water flowing noiselessly from the hillside, and each gentle rivulet, contributes to the formation of the great river that rolls into the ocean—is the clear teaching of the Bible, and may yet be recognized as the equally clear teaching of philosophy. The glory of that rivulet is not that it falls gently down the mountain side, or flows sweetly through the vale, beautiful as that may be, but that it *does* contribute to swell the great river which thus rolls into the ocean. So the glory of a plan or act of man may be, that, though in itself too insignificant to be remembered, it *does* contribute to carry out the great plans of God—the plans that embrace eternity and infinity.

The point to which I am here adverting, that all human plans are made subservient to the accomplishment of a higher Divine purpose, is clearly stated in the Bible. "A man's heart deviseth his way, but the Lord directeth his steps," Prov. xvi. 9. "There are many devices in a man's heart; nevertheless the counsel of the Lord, that shall stand," Prov. xix. 21. "The way of man is not in himself: it is not in man that walketh to direct his steps," Jer. x. 23. "Surely the wrath of man shall praise thee: the remainder of wrath shalt thou restrain," Psa. lxxvi. 10. "I am God, and there is none else: I am God, and there is none like me, declaring the end from the beginning, and from ancient times the things that are not yet done, saying, My counsel shall stand, and I will do all my pleasure," Isa. xlvi. 9, 10. This sentiment has been beautifully expressed also by the great poet,—

> " Our indiscretion sometimes serves us well,
>   When our deep plots do pall ; and that should teach us,
>   There 's a divinity that shapes our ends,
>   Rough-hew them how we will."*

Philosophy has not been willing to avow this as an admitted truth, but *history* is fast tending to it; and the time is not distant when no philosophy will be regarded as complete, as no history is, which does not recognize the idea. No man can furnish a correct explanation of the facts of history, isolated as they seem to be, who does not regard them as part of a vast system, under the superintendence of one Presiding Mind, with one great plan extending over the entire race of man, and embracing all kingdoms, empires, and lands. Each one of the events of the world, isolated as it may appear, becomes thus a part of a comprehensive scheme—entering into the *development* of the Divine purposes as really as the arrangement of the various separate particles in a tree or in the human frame is connected with its development in its perfect form; or as the little labours of the animalculæ become connected with

* Hamlet, act v. sc. 2.

the beautiful formations that rise above the sea in reefs or islands. The individual insect dies and is forgotten; the plan goes steadily forward.

It gives a new view of life in regard to its value, when a man, however humble and obscure he may be, can recognize the Divine hand in his own course through the world, and can see that God has been accomplishing what he himself never contemplated or intended, and what he may himself not even now understand. He himself, like the insect in the formation of the coral reef, may pass away and be forgotten. There may have been nothing in his own work to perpetuate the memory of his individuality; the stone which friendship may erect over his grave may fall down, and the place where he sleeps in death may be unmarked and unknown: but he has become absorbed in a greater 'movement than his own individual plans, and a purpose higher than he has ever designed has been accomplished by his living on the earth.

It may seem to be mere vanity now to apply these remarks in any way to myself, but they are as applicable to one man as another, and they are now so applied only to illustrate this one general point, showing how life seems to a man when he approaches its close. The idea is, that at such a time a man will feel that his life has been shaped otherwise than he

anticipated ; that he has rarely carried out his own
plans ; that he has, in fact, pursued a different course
from that which he or his parents designed ; that he
has failed much in what he intended, and that if he
has accomplished anything, it has been in a great
measure what he neither contemplated nor designed.

I had, when a boy, a young friend—a playmate, a
schoolmate,—he, like myself, being the son of a
mechanic, and neither of us with any other advantage than our other playmates and schoolmates had.
From our early prospects and occupations we were
both turned aside by the suggestions of a country
schoolmaster, who persuaded us, with the somewhat
reluctant assent of our parents, to leave our homes
with a view to a course of studies preparatory to the
profession of the law. My youthful friend, by talent
and industry in the line thus contemplated, placed
himself at the head of the legal profession in our
native state, and ultimately occupied the highest
judicial position in the state, accomplishing a purpose
of which he never dreamed in early life, and illustrating the thought which I am endeavouring to set
before you, that "there's a divinity that shapes our
ends ;" that " a man's heart deviseth his way, but the
Lord directeth his steps."

If it should be said that the case referred to is by
no means an unusual thing ; that it is, in fact, a

matter of common occurrence, I admit that this is so, and it is for this very reason that I have adverted to it. It is to show that it *is* so common, I may say so universal, as to prove that there is over all things, and embracing all things, a great plan; that there is one presiding Intellect over all; that there is a God who has His own purposes, and who makes those of his creatures subordinate to His own; that, in fact, while they are free, He has the power to control them so as to carry out His own designs.

But what I wished particularly to advert to, as pertaining to the matter before us, was, to show how this *appears* to a man who has reached the outer limit of human life, and who from that point looks back over his own course. Few, if any, at that period, can look over life without recalling the fact that they have often been embarrassed in their way; that they have met with many disappointments in their cherished plans; that obstacles from unforeseen quarters have been thrown in their path; nay, that they may have been compelled more than once to change their plans of life. At the time when these things occurred they felt them keenly. They were saddened by disappointment, and wept at their want of success; they felt that even "the stars in their courses fought against them;" they were envious at the success of others in whose path no obstacles seemed to be interposed; and possibly they may have been tempted to murmur at what seemed to them an unjust and a partial government of the world—against that superior Power that gave success to others, and frowned on their path. Now, in the review, however, all this seems to be changed. Those reverses are seen to have been under a wise direction, in order that they who were thus disappointed might accomplish what they had not designed to accomplish, as well as that their own spiritual and eternal good might be secured. So we now look over the history of the world, and see that the great changes which have occurred among the nations—the revolutions of states and empires, the reverses, the judgments, and the calamities which have come upon nations, have all been necessary in the great movements of human affairs, and have all tended in some way to promote the ultimate welfare of man, and to contribute to the progress of the race.

For myself, if it will not be regarded as mere vanity to refer to this, I may say that all this has been illustrated in my own life as it now seems to me in the review of the past. I have carried out none of the purposes of my early years. I have failed in those things which I had designed and which I hoped to accomplish. I have done what I had never purposed or expected to do. I have known what it was to weep at discouragements. I have been led along contrary to my early anticipations. I can now see, I think, that while I have been conscious of entire freedom in all that I have done, yet my whole life has been under the absolute control of a Higher Power, and that there has been a will and a plan in regard to my life which was not my own. Even my most voluntary acts, I can see, have been subservient to that higher plan, and what I have done has been done as if I had no agency in the matter.

It would not be proper to go into details here, and if I did they would be such only as occur substantially in the life of every man, and which any one could recount at the age of seventy. It is not because there has been anything peculiar in my case that I advert to this, but merely to illustrate a general truth—to show you how life will *seem* to you when you review it at its close. If I have done anything in the world, what I have done has been from no original purpose or plan of my own; if praise is due anywhere, it is not to me, but to Him who has directed my steps; if I have been useful in any respect, it is because there was a controlling Providence that directed my path.

But if the personal reference may be allowed, I may allude to what in fact has proved to be the principal work of my life, and that in which I have been more successful than in any other; I mean the preparation of notes or commentaries on the Sacred Scriptures. For this work I had made no special preparation, and it never entered into my early plans or expectations. I was led to it as a *side-work* altogether, and pursued it as a pleasurable occupation from day to day. I began merely with the design of preparing a few plain and simple notes on the Gospels for the benefit of Sunday-school teachers. There was a demand for some brief explanation of the Gospels for Sunday-schools, and it was certain that such a work would be furnished by some one. Three other gentlemen, each of them peculiarly qualified for the task, commenced the preparation of such notes at about the same time, but each of them abandoned the design. With me the preparation of those notes on the Gospels led to the *habit* of spending a small portion of each day in writing on some part of the Bible, at such a time as would not interfere with my regular duties as a pastor, until, to my own surprise, I found myself at the end of the New Testament, and until, to my greater surprise, as the result has shown, more than a million of volumes have been sold in this country and abroad, in my native tongue, and in languages which I cannot read or understand. If there may seem to have been some self-denial required in pursuing such a work for more than thirty years, in doing it in the early morning hours when the inhabitants of this great city were slumbering round about me, in pursuing it when burdened with the duties of a most responsible charge, in going to my study in the early morning in all kinds of weather—cold, heat, storm, rain, snow—if there seems to have been something like dogged perseverance in this—I would say that this does not appear to me now to be so. Nothing is plainer to my own apprehension, nothing more indelibly impressed on my mind in the review of the past, than that there was an unseen Hand that guided me in this work from day to day, and an influence from above that prompted me to it; that there was a demand in the state of the church that it should be done by some one; that an emergency had arisen in the establishment of a new institution, the Sunday-school, for such a work; that God gave me health, and strength, and a love for the work with reference to its accomplishment; that He awoke me morning by morning for the pleasant task; that His hand guided my own in writing; and that, although conscious of being entirely voluntary, there was an over-ruling Providence, an overruling *Power*, that prompted to the conception of the task, and that led to its completion.

I am constrained now to ask you to forgive this personal allusion — this reference in this public manner to my own labours. As I know my own heart, it is not in any spirit of boasting; it is only that I may now, at the end of my labours on earth, render the praise where the praise is due, and that I may illustrate a great truth of value to all, that "a man's heart deviseth his way," but that "the counsel of the Lord, that shall stand;" that there is a supreme providence; that there is a God who rules over human affairs; that there is a great comprehensive plan to which all our plans are subordinate. I have no claim to merit, to praise, or to honour, on account of what I have been enabled to do. I refer to it now with no such view. I am trying to show to those in earlier life how a man feels when he has reached the outer limits of his course; and what I wish to say is, that it then seems to him that there has been a Divine hand in his course, and that his own plans, often frustrated, and whether successful or not, have all been subordinate to a much higher plan, in which all his purposes are absorbed and lost, and in which all that he does may be, in view of that vast plan, wholly insignificant.

It is a great truth, confirmed more and more in the history of the world, that God *will* make the individual plans of men, and the purposes of nations, subservient to His own. Whether they design it or not, He will make all their schemes subordinate to

that higher and vaster movement which is going forward in the history of the earth; as, also, He will
make all the movements of the earth itself subordinate to the development of that vaster plan which
embraces all worlds, making the universe one.

Life becomes great only when it is contemplated in
connection with the purposes of an overruling Providence—with that scheme which comprehends all
things. Men are great only, when, in their rise and
fall, they are regarded as connected with such a vast
and comprehensive plan. Individuals and nations
have their own purposes and plans. They are alike
voluntary. They may be, or may not be, successful
in their schemes. They alike pass away; they alike
may be forgotten; but the great plan moves on.
That, amidst the failures or the successes of other
plans, is certain to be accomplished. "My covenant
shall stand, and I will do all my pleasure," is the
language of God, alike in His word and in the course
of events.

The individual workers pass away. The countless
millions of the toilers on the earth disappear. The
actors of other times, the builders of the pyramids,
the hosts that composed the armies of Xerxes, Cyrus,
Alexander, Cæsar, have all vanished. The builders
of Thebes, of Nineveh, of Babylon, of Rome, have all
gone. The great orators, lawgivers, poets, conquerors,

sages, philosophers, are withdrawn. The grave has closed over them; but the results of their conflicts, their toils, their genius, have gone into the history of the world, with God's greater plan that embraces and comprehends all. So the nations themselves pass away. Egypt, Assyria, the Grecian states, the Roman empire, the kingdoms that Alexander founded, the kingdoms of the Huns, the Goths, the Vandals—of Attila and Tamerlane—have passed away; but they were great in their history, because their rise and fall were parts of one comprehensive plan which embraces all people and all times, and which, when those parts are combined, will make the history of this world truly *great.*

III.

SHALL now advert to a point which seems not improper to be dwelt upon by one who has reached the period of threescore and ten. It is, that *it is a much greater thing to have lived through these seventy years just past than it was to have lived through any previous seventy years in the world's history.* A similar remark, I have no doubt, will be made, and with much more force and propriety, by one who shall live through the next seventy years, and with still greater force and propriety in advancing periods of the world; but the remark has now a force which it could never have had before our time.

I mean by the remark that it has been a greater privilege to live during these seventy years than it would have been to live any seventy years previous to this period; that life has been worth more; that there have been more advantages for securing the great ends of living; that there has been more that a man could do; that life has been practically much *longer,* and that the responsibilities of living have been proportionally greater.

[1.] There have been times and countries (and there are still), where seventy years of human existence are of very little value. In such times and countries, the world makes no progress. It is substantially the same at the beginning and the close of the period. There is no accumulation of wealth, of influence, of learning. In savage life the same style of living prevails; the tents, huts, or houses are built in the same manner; the same modes of hunting, of fishing, or of cultivating the ground exist; the same manner of dress; the same modes of travel; the same kinds of amusement or pastime; the same rules of administering to the maladies of the sick; the same methods of war, and the same ideas in regard to the objects of living. Seventy years of savage life— what is it worth? The savage makes no progress, for his life at the beginning of such a period and at its close is the same.

This is also true in regard to nations which have emerged in some degree from savage life, and which have attained to a considerable degree of civilization. Seventy years of life in Egypt when the pyramids were built—what were they worth? Seventy years in the middle ages in Europe—what were they worth? When, under the best circumstances, and with the highest aims, whole years of patient toil were to be spent in transcribing a volume of Plato or Aristotle, in copying the Sacred Scriptures, or in substituting the legend of a saint for one of the obliterated books of Livy, how much could be made of such a life? Seventy years in China now—seventy years at any period within three thousand years in China—what are they, what have they been worth? China, thousands of years ago, reached the highest point of civilization possible under the existing form of its institutions and its religion, and progress there is impossible until there shall be some great revolution. Life there three thousand years ago, for all the purposes pertaining to this world or the world to come, was as valuable as it is now. A citizen of that nation can make no more of it now than he could have made then, and whether he lived at the one period or the other might have been a matter of perfect indifference.

[2.] But seventy years of life may be much more important, and may for all the purposes of living, be much longer at one period of the world than another. It is much more so now than it ever was or could be among savage tribes; than it was in Ancient Egypt or Assyria; than it was or is in India or in China; than it was in Scotland, in England, in France, or in Germany, previous to the Reformation; nay, than it was in our own country during the last century. It will be vastly more momentous and valuable—

immensely *longer* in respect to all that can be made of life—in the next seventy years than it is now.

In most important respects the discoveries which have been made in our own times—the inventions and improvements in the arts of living—have been equivalent to making life twice, or thrice, or four times as long as it once was, or of adding twice, or thrice, or four times to the duration of human existence on earth. A man whose business is to travel, who can pass over as much in his journey now in one hour as would on a camel, or on a horse, or on foot, have occupied twelve hours, has in this respect added eleven hours in such a journey to his life. In former times it required the slow labour of a monk two or three years to transcribe the Bible—a work which can now be performed by the art of printing in a few hours, including on an average, all the labour of type-setting, and stereotyping, of folding and of binding; and thus, just so much has been added to the life of man. In the best days of Greece or of Rome, or in Arabia under the caliphs, or in the dark ages, an author might acquire celebrity who could send out a thousand copies of a work of his own, or secure their circulation; in this age a man may send out in different languages a million of volumes of his own to influence for good or for evil, the people of his own or foreign lands. So much *may* life be worth now as compared with former times.

The same is true with regard to the machines for mowing, and reaping, and thrashing,—for carding, and spinning, and weaving,—for the communication of intelligence by letters, by the telegraph, and by newspapers,—for the purposes of travel and navigation,—for the transfer of the products of the earth to market;—for the manufacture of raw materials into the forms that they are designed to assume in clothing, in coin, in structures of utility or ornament,—in everything that ministers to domestic comfort or to public welfare. Any one may see the force of this remark if he will estimate the influence of the sewing-machine—an invention of our own age,—and if he will calculate how much has been added to female life by this most ingenious invention, abridging by more than one-half this portion of the labours of a family.

All this is equivalent to making life as many times longer, for all the purposes of wealth, of happiness, and of knowledge, as has been saved by machinery and inventions. The unconscious powers of nature now accomplish a large part of what *was* done by human muscles, and do it better than it could have been done by the unaided hand of man. The mere lengthening of life to the period of Methuselah would not in itself be equivalent to what has been gained in this manner; and for all the purposes of living, human life is now incomparably longer than it was in the time of the antediluvian patriarchs. The *aggregate*, so to speak, of human existence, is thus vast;—more vast by far than it would have been to have *added* these years now saved to life in ruder periods of the world; for a man can accomplish incomparably more now than he could have done in other ages by any mere addition of days or years. The addition of a hundred years to the life of a monk would only have enabled him to transcribe a few more copies of the Bible—which can now be produced in a few moments. The addition of any number of years to the life of the builders of the pyramids would only have enabled them to pile a few more stones on the vast mass. The addition of any number of years to the life of a savage would have left him a savage still, and with nothing accomplished —with no advance towards civilization—with no accumulation of property or knowledge. The addition of any number of years to the life of an inhabitant of China would contribute little or nothing to the real duration of his life.

[3.] This is a different world from what it was seventy years ago. The universe, if I may so express it, is larger than it was then; the earth is more ancient and more grand. It is true, indeed, that to the eye of an Omniscient Being the universe is the same; but it is more vast as it appears to man. Every seventy years of the earth's history, except perhaps the period of the dark ages, has made the world different; but no period of seventy years has made so great a change as that to which I now refer. There is not a science whose boundaries have not been greatly enlarged. Many of the most important discoveries in science, and inventions in the arts, which are to be developed in their influence on following ages, have started into being in groups and clusters. Worlds and systems have been brought into view unknown to man before.

The universe *above* is greater. During all that period, the astronomer has been pointing his telescope to the heavens, and penetrating the fields of blue ether, and revealing to man the wonders of the distant heavens; enlarging the universe by all those measureless distances through which the eye has been made to penetrate. New stars have been discovered and mapped on the great chart of the heavens; a new planet as belonging to our system has been found from the fact of its disturbing influence on those before known—a planet on which no human eye ever before rested; a vast number of asteroids, fragments of a larger planet, have been seen to revolve between the orbit of Mars and Jupiter; and distant nebulæ, floating islands in the measureless distance, have been brought into view, and resolved into distinct and separate worlds.

The world *beneath* is greater and more wonderful than it was. The microscope was indeed known, as was the telescope, seventy years ago; but it had just begun to reveal the world beneath us. It has not finished its work, but it has already disclosed a universe beneath us as unlimited and as wonderful as that above us. It has peopled every leaf in the forest, and every drop of water in rivulets, lakes, and oceans, with teeming multitudes of inhabitants, amazing us as much by their number, and by the delicacy, skill, and beauty of their organization, as the telescope does by the number and the magnitudes of the worlds above us. We find ourselves standing thus in a universe extending illimitably above and below us, as incomprehensible on the one hand as on the other: boundless space above filled up with worlds, where we thought there was an empty void; and beneath, countless myriads of beings starting into life and playing their little part, where all seemed to be blank.

Our own earth is vaster and more grand than it was. Half a century ago, the prevailing—the almost universal—belief was, that the earth was created six

thousand years ago, in its essential structure as it is
now—rocks, and seas, and rivers, and hills having
been called into existence as they now are, by the
immediate command of God. It began, indeed, to
be whispered that it is older, and that important
changes had occurred upon the earth before man
appeared on it; or that the earth had a history
before the history of the human race. I remember in
one of the earliest stages of my education, meeting
with a remark by Dr. Chalmers, designed to solve
some of the growing difficulties from the new science
of geology, that between the first and second verses
of the book of Genesis there might be supposed to
have intervened an indefinite period of which no
account was given, the purpose of inspiration having
been first to attest the general truth that *"God
created the heavens and the earth,"* or to secure this
belief in the minds of men in opposition to the idea
that the world is eternal, or is the work of fate or
chance, and then, without detailing the intermediate
history of the globe, to proceed at once to the main
purpose of the volume, the history of the creation,
the fall, and the redemption of man; that in fact
the earth itself may have existed through a vast
number of ages, and may have gone through an
immense number of revolutions, with which man in
his history was not particularly concerned, or which

did not bear on the main purpose of the volume—the
record of the fall and recovery of a lost race.   What
was then almost conjecture in regard to the past
history of the earth, has been verified.   The prevailing opinions respecting its recent origin have
been set aside.   To all that was before regarded as
grand in the conception of the earth, there is now
added the belief that it has moved on its axis and in
its orbit millions of ages; that successive generations
of animals have been formed, and have acted out the
purpose of their creation, and have disappeared for
ever; that vast changes have occurred in the waters
and on the land, displacing each other, and peopled
again with new myriads of inhabitants appropriate to
each, and then again to pass away; that immense
deposits of minerals had been made by the slow
progress of ages, fitted for the use of an order of
beings that had not yet appeared; and that at last
man, to whom all these changes had reference, and
for whom all the previous arrangements were designed, appeared upon the earth, a being of higher
order—the last in the series that was to occupy the
globe.   With this view of the past, what a different
object is the earth now from what it was seventy
years ago !

A large part of the discoveries in science, the
inventions in the arts, and the arrangements in the

schemes of benevolence that are to affect future times, and whose bearings can now be scarcely appreciated, has been originated also in this period of the world. The power of steam was not indeed unknown before; but the great changes which it is destined to produce in the commerce of the world are the results of the inventions of this age. The railroad and the magnetic telegraph have been originated in these times. Every science has been pushed forward. Elementary books of instruction have been changed, and those which were adapted to the condition of the world seventy years ago would be useless now. If I were now to begin my education again, a large part of the books which I studied when young would be valueless. I should, indeed, retain my Homer, my Virgil, and my Euclid; but the books in which I sought instruction in chemistry and geography and natural philosophy, would no longer represent the science of the world, or convey correct views to my mind. The books which I then studied belong to another age, and though they will serve to mark the steps by which the advances of science have been made, they will never again be a proper exponent of the true state of knowledge among mankind. I see wonders around me which have sprung up anew. Every river, lake, and ocean is navigated by steam; an iron road is laid down everywhere, connecting all parts of a country together, along which are borne, by a power unapplied when I was young, the productions of agriculture, manufactures, and the arts, with a rapidity and a precision of which no one then could have formed a conception. A mysterious and incomprehensible network, like spiders' webs, is weaving itself over all lands, and making its way beneath deep waters, by which thought is transmitted simultaneously to millions of minds, and is diffused over distant lands regardless of mountains and of oceans. How different such a world from what it was seventy years ago !

In the same time there have sprung also into being arrangements, then unknown, no less adapted to affect the moral and religious condition of mankind. The great enterprises of Christian benevolence, yet to result in the entire conversion of the world to God, have been originated in that time. The Bible was indeed in men's hands, and the gospel was preached, and the power of the press was known; but the serious thought had scarcely found its way into the minds of the friends of the Saviour, of bringing the combined influence of these agencies on the widest scale possible to bear on the unconverted portions of the race. Within the period of which I am now speaking, this thought has taken a firm possession of the Christian mind and heart, and the great work of the world's conversion has been entered on in earnest. The Bible has been translated into nearly all the languages of the world; the strongholds of the earth have been occupied as missionary stations; millions of children are taught the great truths of Christianity from week to week in Sabbath-schools; and a Christian literature is spreading its influence far and near over nominally Christian and Pagan lands. Whatever there is of power in these arrangements as bearing on the future, is the fruit of the spirit of this age; and now, in reference to science, to the arts, to the efforts of benevolence—to the world above, the world below, the world in the past, and the world around us, the man of threescore years and ten sees a far different, a much *larger world* than it was when he began to live.

[4.] If now we take into consideration this idea of the vast enlargement of the boundaries of all knowledge during the past period of seventy years,—if we remember how different the world is from what it was at the commencement of that period,—if we call to our recollection what has been done in the way of discovery and invention during that period,—if we remember how much more of the earth has been explored and peopled during that period,—if we think of the disclosures made by the telescope in the worlds above us, or by the microscope in the worlds beneath us,—if we think of the advances in the sciences, in the arts, and in the arrangements of the schemes of benevolence that are to affect future times, and to determine the condition of the world in far-distant ages,—if we attempt to follow out the bearings of the use of steam in manufactures and in commerce by land and by sea,—if we could estimate the influence of the magnetic telegraph on the affairs of nations,—if we could place ourselves back at the year eighteen hundred, and look at the world as it was then, in contrast with what it is now, we might form some estimate of what it has been to have lived during these seventy years, and some faint conception of what are and must be the privileges and responsibilities of those who, instead of *ending* life, are about to *start off* from life's beginning on the more glorious periods of the next seventy years : for to all human appearance, and beyond all question, the next seventy years will be more remarkable in the progress of discovery, in the development of the human powers, in the diffusion of the principles of liberty, and in the spread of the true religion, than any past period of the world. If one about to leave the world might shrink from its responsibilities in living in such a period as that which is to succeed the present, yet he might be pardoned for being conscious, as I am, of a strong desire to witness the glory, the honour, and the progress of my native land, of the church, and of the world, in such a coming age. There has never been a period when the prospects of the future were so bright and glorious; there has never been a period when, to a man on the verge of the grave, such a desire could have been so natural or so pardonable, or when the regret at leaving the world could have been so profound.

Our own country furnishes a better illustration of the thought which I am presenting than any other portion of the world. The period of threescore and ten years to which I am now adverting, began at the death of Washington, and when the effects of his illustrious services and the principles of his policy were just beginning to develop themselves. A new nation was just founded. A new and but partially tried Constitution had been adopted. The experiment of self-government had not yet been fully tried. There were many doubts and many misgivings about the working of the new government under any circumstances; there were more doubts as to the question whether the form of government could be adapted to a nation of many millions—to vast and numerous states with very varied interests—to a population spreading over a continent. There were then sixteen states in the Union. There was a population of scarcely five millions. A narrow strip of territory on the Atlantic coast, scarcely now appreciable on a map, had been subdued and cultivated. There were a few small commercial towns—what would now be called *villages*—Charleston, Baltimore, Philadelphia, New York, Boston, on that coast. The great West had not been explored even by the most hardy travellers. California, Oregon, Nevada, Nebraska, Minnesota, Kansas, were as much unknown as is now the centre of Africa. If I remember right, Mr. Monroe (when President) recommended that the vast and fertile lands of what now constitutes the state of Iowa, should be appropriated as a reservation to the Indian tribes, as a region so remote that it would not be likely to be invaded and disturbed by the progress of civilization. No one could then anticipate what seventy years were to produce in our country under any ordinary system of development then known; still less could any one have anticipated the new powers which would be brought into existence for navigating our rivers and lakes, for conveying intelligence, for facilitating commerce, for the development of the vast unknown resources of the land. That same nation now—what is it as compared with what it was then! What a history has been the history of these seventy years! What a place will that history occupy in the general history of the world! What a nation is this as compared with what it was at the end of the last century! And though a man may himself have taken no part in these great movements, though he may have contributed nothing to make his country what it is, though he will soon pass away and his name never be remembered,—yet, any one who has lived through this period may be pardoned for self-congratulation that the beginning and the close of his life embrace such a period, and for finding satisfaction in the thought that he has been permitted to witness the developments of these seventy years. He who loves his country may rejoice in the thought that he has seen it pass safely through the times of its greatest danger; that when, as soon he must, he closes his eyes on human things, he will see that country free in every part, and in reference to every one of its citizens; that he will see a constitution which has been put to the utmost test, and which has been found equal to the test; that he will see a government which in respect to vigour and adaptedness to a vast territory equals the hopes of the most sanguine, and surpasses the expectations of most of its founders; that he will see one great united people, destined, in all human probability, to accomplish more for the good of man than all the nations of antiquity have done, or than is to be accomplished by any existing people on the globe.

IV.

HAVE spoken of the past as the past now appears to me. It remains that I should say a few words of *the future* from the same point of view,—near the close of what is commonly regarded as a long life. It would be a proper question for any one to ask of a man who has reached that age,—who may have been for half a century occupied in public life,— whose position has given him an opportunity of extensive observation and of intercourse with the world,—who has passed that time in a period when the world has undergone more important changes, and made more rapid progress than at any former period,—whose professional calling has made it his duty to acquaint himself with books and with the opinions that prevail in his time on morals, philosophy, and religion—how the world seems in regard to the future. Is it dark and gloomy, or is it bright and hopeful? Is it growing better or worse? Is there hope for the future, or is the mind overwhelmed with sad forebodings? Has the world made progress, or is it in a retrograde movement? Is there hope

for those in earlier life—hope for their country, hope for the church, hope for the interests of religion, of humanity, of liberty? Does it seem now that all that cheered in the days of youth, and that prompted to generous aspirations then, was illusive, false, and vain? Could a man, with the experience of seventy years, now enter on life with any bright hopes of the future—with anything to stimulate and animate in reference to the prospects of the race? These are fair questions for any one to ask. He who has reached the period of threescore and ten, *ought* to be able to answer them.

It cannot be denied, as I have already remarked, that there are aged men who see nothing but darkness and gloom in the prospects of mankind; who feel that the world is much worse than it was when they looked out on it in youth, full of hope; who despair of any permanent reformation of the race, and of the removal of existing evils by any means that man can employ, or by any developement of principles already existing, and who look for the removal of those evils only by some new and miraculous Divine manifestation; who anticipate that the world is to become worse until the necessity of such intervention shall become apparent to all men in the utter failure of all human efforts at improvement and reform. Nor can it be denied that there are many in early life who suppose that these are the common

F

views and feelings of old men; that aged men are necessarily peevish, disappointed, soured, and melancholy; and that, whatever may have been their early hopes in regard to the world, their sun is setting amid thick clouds and darkness. Is this necessarily so? Have aged men no better views or prospects than these to set before those who are to succeed them on the great theatre of human affairs?

These questions naturally divide themselves into two parts, or relate to two subjects: *First,* how a man at "threescore and ten" regards the future prospects of this world. *Second,* how he himself feels in regard to the future state, or what are his hopes in reference to that world on which he is so soon to enter.

For very obvious reasons there would be an impropriety in referring in this manner to the latter. The remarks which I shall make, therefore, will pertain only to the former.

The opinion which I shall express may have little value in itself. It will show, however, that an aged man *may* take cheerful views of life, of the world, of the certain progress of the race, of the destiny of man. What, then, are the prospects of the world in regard to the future?

I look at two things;—at the predictions in the Bible; and at the course of events, as tending to the fulfilment of those predictions.

1. *The predictions in the Bible.* Believing, as I have believed for fifty years, that the Bible is a revelation from God, and confirmed more and more, as I have been, in that belief by the study of that volume for more than forty years, I naturally turn to it alike in reference to the future condition of this world, and to my own hopes. I find there, as pertaining to the prospects of the world, such statements as the following: "The wilderness and the solitary place shall be glad, and the desert shall rejoice and blossom as the rose," Isa. xxxv. 1. "The wolf shall dwell with the lamb, and the leopard shall lie down with the kid; and the calf, and the young lion, and the fatling together; and a little child shall lead them. They shall not hurt nor destroy in all my holy mountain; for the earth shall be full of the knowledge of the Lord, as the waters cover the sea," Isa. xi. 6—9. "Violence shall no more be heard in thy land, wasting nor destruction within thy borders; but thou shalt call thy walls Salvation, and thy gates Praise. The sun shall be no more thy light by day; neither for brightness shall the moon give light unto thee: but the Lord shall be unto thee an everlasting light, and thy God thy glory. Thy sun shall no more go down; neither shall thy moon withdraw itself: for the Lord shall be thine everlasting light, and the days of thy mourning shall be ended. Thy gates

shall be opened continually; they shall not be shut day nor night; that men may bring unto thee the forces of the Gentiles, and that their kings may be brought," Isa. lx. 11, 18—21. "Unto us a Child is born, unto us a Son is given; and the government shall be upon His shoulder: and His name shall be called Wonderful, Counsellor, The mighty God, The everlasting Father, The Prince of Peace. Of the increase of His government and peace there shall be no end, upon the throne of David, and upon his kingdom, to order it, and to establish it with judgment and with justice, from henceforth even for ever," Isa. ix. 6, 7. "He shall have dominion also from sea to sea, and from the river unto the ends of the earth. In His days shall the righteous flourish; and abundance of peace so long as the moon endureth. His name shall endure for ever: His name shall be continued as long as the sun; and men shall be blessed in Him: all nations shall call Him blessed," Psa. lxxii. 7, 8, 17. "I saw in the night visions, and, behold, one like the Son of man came with the clouds of heaven, . . . and there was given Him dominion, and glory, and a kingdom, that all people, nations, and languages should serve Him; His dominion is an everlasting dominion, which shall not pass away, and His kingdom that which shall not be destroyed; and the kingdom and dominion, and the greatness of the kingdom under the whole heaven, shall be given to the people of the saints of the Most High," Dan. vii. 13, 14, 27.

To such a time, when peace and righteousness and prosperity and knowledge and pure religion shall pervade the earth, all the prophecies in the Sacred Scriptures undoubtedly tend. No one can close the perusal of the Bible without the feeling that, according to that book, the time is coming when universal peace will prevail on the earth, and when the true religion, with all its unspeakable blessings, will pervade the world. The prophetic writers, many of whom were aged men, and many of whom had experienced much of the depravity of the world, and many of whom had lived in time of crime and disaster, were not gloomy, sad, dispirited, morose, and disappointed men. No men have ever lived who have cherished brighter views of the future condition of man ; no heathen sages or philosophers were so cheerful and hopeful when they looked onward to the future state of the world. How *can* a man who believes that book, and who confides in those predictions, look with dark and sad forebodings on the future ? How *can* he believe that the affairs of men are destined constantly to grow worse ?

2. *The course of events.* I believe that this

coincides now with the predictions in the Bible in regard to the future in our world. I think I see indications that human affairs are tending to that state when science, liberty, justice, pure morals, and the Christian religion will pervade the earth; when all those predictions in the sacred volume will be accomplished.

(1.) In the progress of human affairs nothing is lost that is of value. We have all now that was valuable in Egyptian, Grecian, Roman, Alexandrian, or Arabian civilization, alike in their philosophy, their science, their arts, their jurisprudence, their principles of freedom. Nothing that was ever of value to mankind has been lost; there is nothing which has been lost by which the world would now be the gainer, if it could be recovered; there is nothing which has been dropped which has not been superseded by something better, and superseded by it *because* it is better. In like manner, nothing can hereafter destroy those great improvements and inventions which have contributed so much to the world's progress in our time. Combined with that which the past has transmitted to us, these things go into that vast accumulation of forces which are to mould and bless the world in all time to come. What can now destroy the printing-press, the telescope, the microscope, the railroad, the steamboat, the magnetic telegraph? What can now obliterate from the memory of mankind those great principles of justice, of liberty, and of law, which enter into modern civilization?

(2.) The old systems that have tyrannized over men have lost their power, and have died out, or are dying out never to be revived. This is true alike in religion and in all forms of civil government.

(*a.*) IN RELIGION. The systems of *ancient Paganism* have died out never to be revived. There is not now on the earth a worshipper of the ancient gods of Babylon, of Egypt, of Greece, or of Rome; and not one of the temples erected for their worship will be rebuilt or repaired. The temple of Bel in Babylon, the magnificent structures in Thebes, the Parthenon at Athens, and the Pantheon at Rome, are desolate for ever so far as the design for which they were raised is concerned; nor is there now, nor will there be hereafter, a single human being who will ever offer a bloody sacrifice there, or cast a grain of incense on their altars. All that there was in those religions to degrade mankind, or to pander to vice, has passed away never to be revived.

The same is true of the *existing* systems of Paganism. Whatever may be the power or influence of such systems on the world up to a certain period in society, a time comes when that power ceases, and when they show themselves not to be adapted to an advanced period of the world. It might be difficult to *prove* that the systems of Paganism in the Babylonian Empire, in Egypt, in Greece, or in Rome, materially interfered with the civilization of those states and kingdoms up to the point which they actually reached; it might, in like manner, be difficult to *prove* that the systems of Brahminism or Buddhism have interfered with the civilization of India or China up to the point which they have reached; but it is clear that neither could be adapted to a higher civilization; in other words, that if the sciences and arts existing in Europe should be transferred to India or China, those religions must vanish. They cannot be adjusted to that state of higher development, but must retard and oppose it. They have had their day, and have exhausted themselves, and are destined to lose their hold on the world, whatever may succeed them. They are destined to *die out*, as have the old systems of Babylon and Rome.

The same is true of the *Papal* power. It has had its day. Does any one *now* believe that the power which was wielded over the nations of Europe by Gregory vii., by Innocent iii., or by Boniface viii., can be revived? Can the power of dethroning kings and of laying kingdoms under an interdict be restored? Will the time come again when princes will turn pale on their thrones, and nations tremble, at the threatening of an Italian priest? Can the Inquisition be revived again in the world? Is there to be another Philip II.? another duke of Alva to drench whole provinces in the blood of martyrs? another Mary to light again the fires of Smithfield? To ask these questions is to answer them.*

(*b.*) IN MATTERS OF CIVIL GOVERNMENT. The old dynasties that tyrannized over man have likewise passed away, never to be re-established. The tendency in civil affairs is everywhere to liberty, to equality, to the overthrow of the old systems of tyranny; to the establishment of institutions founded on the rights of man. Can the days of Nero, of Caligula, of Philip II., of Richard III., and of Henry VIII. return again? Would such men be permitted now to occupy any of the thrones of earth? No. Those days have passed. The scenes which occurred under those reigns are not to be renewed. There is a spirit abroad in the world—IN ALL THE WORLD—which would prevent it; and the bloody scenes of civil tyranny, as well as of fiery religious persecution, pertain to the past. Whatever may occur, the future historian will have no such deeds to record, and the

---

* For a full illustration and proof of this point, compare Hallam's ' View of the State of Europe during the Middle Ages,' vol. i. chap. 7, pp. 402-496.

catalogue of monsters on thrones is filled up. Nations would combine against such, and fleets and armies would hasten to hurl them from their thrones.

(3.) I look at the accumulation of the *forces* now in existence in favour of progress, of order, of law, of liberty, of just government, of the rights of man, of truth, of religion.

Those forces consist of all the discoveries and inventions of ancient and modern times; of all that has been accomplished in the arts, in philosophy, in jurisprudence, in medicine, in law, in political science, in theology; of the recorded results of all the profound thinking of the great intellects of the world; of all that constitutes modern civilization; of all that tends to progress in agriculture and the mechanic arts; of all the arrangements for domestic comfort; and of all that enters into the merchandise and commerce of the nations of the earth. It is to be remembered that the tendency of each and all these things is to elevate, and not to debase and degrade mankind; that each and all move the world forward and not backward, It is to be remembered, also, that all these things are really connected with the interests and happiness of mankind, and that the world will sooner or later perceive this, and act on the idea; for nothing is plainer than that industry, temperance, justice, honesty, truth, charity, knowledge,—that all the virtues, including all that there is in true religion, really coincide with the prosperity and happiness of nations and individuals, nay, that they are essential to prosperity and happiness. The world, slow in learning it, is beginning to see this. It will ultimately perceive it clearly. Men will not always be blind to their own real interests; and all these things, therefore, constitute a vast accumulation of *forces*—the gathered results of ages—bearing on the future welfare of the race, and making certain the future prosperity and happiness of the world.

(4.) I look, then, at the accumulation of these things in their relation to Christianity, and to the probability of its prevalence in the world. It might be shown, I think, that this is the only existing form of religion that *promises* to be permanent on the earth, or that if there is to be ultimately a *universal* religion, this is the only one that would be adapted to such universality in the higher forms of progress to which the race will rise. As I have already remarked, the ancient systems will not be revived; and there is no one of the existing forms of heathenism that is making progress *against* Christianity; no one, in fact, that is not silently melting away before it.

But this is not precisely the idea which I am now submitting to your consideration. It is, that those things to which I have referred as *forces* acting on society and on the world, have a close—I believe an *essential*—connexion with Christianity. They become incorporated with it. They go with it. They carry Christianity with themselves wherever they go. For, those things which now most mark the progress of the world, have been originated in close connexion with Christianity; if not directly *by* it, yet in connexion *with* it, and under its fostering care. The art of printing, the mariner's needle for any practical purposes, the labour-saving machines, steam, the magnetic telegraph, the improvements in naval architecture, the comforts of domestic life, the telescope, the microscope—these, and similar things, have either been originated by Christianity, or have grown up with it, and are identified with it, and go forth with it wherever it is diffused. They are *to be* connected, and not to be separated, in all time to come.

It is to be borne in mind, also, that the commerce of the world is mainly in the hands of Christian nations, and, for the most part, is conducted by *Protestant* nations. A Chinese or a Hindoo ship never crosses the ocean for purposes of commerce; Africa sends forth no vessels for commercial purposes, except those which have been built or bought by a Christian colony; savage islands send forth none;

and few are those, and those not increasing, which sail from Roman-catholic ports—from Spain, or Portugal, or Italy, or Brazil, or Austria—from any Roman-catholic ports save those of France. The tendencies of trade and commerce are' to spread the Christian religion; to impress the world with the value of that religion; to open the way for its diffusion; to secure its diffusion in the best and purest form in which that religion exists—in the form of Protestantism. No one, it seems to me, can doubt what is to be the ultimate result of these great movements on the destinies of man.

(5.) From this point the world will not go back. Can we believe that from all this the world is to recede to the savage state; that the experience of the past is to be of no value in regard to the future; that the race is to *relapse* into barbarism; that the world is deliberately to prefer the state of society which existed before Greece and Rome were civilized—the civilization of the middle ages in Europe, or the low state of civilization in India or China—to that which exists in Germany, in France, in England, in the United States of America? What is to become of the printing press; of the telegraph; of the machinery now driven by steam; of observatories; of the telescope; of the microscope; of the mariner's compass; of the quadrant; of reaping machines, and mowing machines, and sewing machines? What is to become of the works of Bacon, and Newton, and Shakespeare, and Milton? What is to become of the treatise of Adam Smith on the Wealth of Nations? What is to become of our school books? What is to become of the Bible? No. These things are not to be lost to the world. They constitute a defence against the return of ignorance, of despotism, of slavery, of superstition, of the Inquisition, of savage barbarity. All this accumulation of forces tends in one direction. Experience, science, the wisdom of the past, commerce, inventions in the arts, all are connected with law and order: with peace and prosperity; with liberty and the rights of man. They are never to be identified with ancient pagan systems of religion revived, or with modern pagan systems; with universal anarchy; with tyranny; with slavery; with scepticism. They will have their widest prevalence, and their most far-reaching influence, only when the Christian religion shall pervade the world.

And can a man, looking at these things, be gloomy, doubtful, disappointed, sad, in reference to the future condition of the world? Shall he close his life in darkness and despair in regard to the earth which he is about to leave? *Can* he who has lived seventy years 'at such an eventful period as this,—who has marked the progress of things for that long course of years,—who compares the present with what the world was when he entered on life—*can* such a man be desponding, gloomy, sad? And can or should a young man who looks out on the world on which *he* is about to enter, look forward only to the loss of all these things, and to anticipated disorder, darkness, augmented crime, and anarchy? Does he enter on a field where there is nothing to cheer and animate him in honourable efforts for the good of mankind? No, no. Never in the history of the world did young men enter on their career with so much to cheer them, to animate them, to inspire them with hope, to call forth their highest powers for the promotion of the great objects which enter into the civilization, the progress, and the happiness of man.

The opinions of a man at seventy years of age have been long maturing, and he is not likely, materially, to change them. I shall cherish these views till I die, and I shall close my eyes in death with bright and glorious hopes in regard to my native land, to the church, and to the world at large; I hope and trust, also, with a more bright and glorious hope in reference to the world to which I shall go.

My work for good or for evil is done. I cannot go back and repair what has been amiss; I cannot now do what has been left undone; I cannot do in a better manner what has been imperfectly performed; I cannot recover the hours that have been wasted; I cannot correct the evils which may have resulted from my errors; I cannot overtake and arrest what I have spoken or written, as it has gone out into the world; I cannot summon back the opportunities for usefulness which have been neglected; I cannot obliterate the reality or the memory of wrong thoughts, or wrong motives, or wrong words, or wrong actions. All that has been thought or said or done in these seventy years has become fixed as a reality, never now to be changed. Past errors and follies may be forgiven, but they are never to be changed. The hope of a man at seventy years of age —at any age—is not that the errors, and sins, and follies of the past can be changed: it is only that they may be pardoned by a merciful God; that they may be covered over by the blood of the atonement; that though they must remain for ever *as facts*—facts fully known to the Great Searcher of hearts—their guilt may be so taken away that they will not be punished; that by the blood shed on the cross they themselves may be so *covered* over—so hidden—that they will not be disclosed on the final trial before assembled worlds. That hope the religion of Christ offers to all. But to all it is *a fact* that life, in all its thoughts, words, actions, becomes *fixed and unchangeable*, as it passes along—as if a river should become *petrified* as its waters flow on towards the ocean, whether its waters be pure or impure, clear or turbid—fixed with all that they bear on their surface, or carry forward in their deep volume. How different would men try to make their lives, if they felt habitually that all—literally all—that they do, or say, or think—even their most fugitive thought—becomes thus fixed and unchangeable *for ever*.

All men are imperfect; and a man when so near the end feels this more sensibly than he does at an earlier period. This will be now his true, his only real consolation—not that he has any merit of his own; not that he has performed any works of righteousness which deserve the Divine favour; not that he has made up at one time of life, or in one form of duty, what he has failed to do in another; not that his imperfections have been so trivial or unimportant that they might easily be overlooked by a just God, or that they would not in themselves exclude him from the Divine favour; not that he might hope for salvation on the ground of his own character, notwithstanding these imperfections: no, no, none of these things, for no well-founded hope of heaven *ever rests* on these grounds;—but only on the ground that his sins, and imperfections, and errors, have *not* been so great, *could not* be so great, as to make it im-

possible for him to be saved by the mercy of God
through the atonement of Christ; that the merits of
the Redeemer are above all the demerits of our sins,
and are ample to save from those sins; that the pro-
visions for pardon and salvation are as free as they
are ample—as available as they are vast; that Christ
"tasted death for every man;" that the offers of
salvation are made to one as well as to another—
made so freely to all, that "whosoever will," may
come and "take the water of life." The hope of man,
of any and of every man, in my sober judgment, (and
I would utter it with all the solemnity which can be
derived from my time of life, and from the fact that
I am not far from the grave,) is found alone in "the
blood of Jesus Christ," which "cleanseth from ALL
SIN."

But the view which a man is constrained to take
of himself as a sinner when he reviews the past, need
not prevent him from cherishing grateful reflections
in regard to his general course of life, or from finding
happiness in the consciousness that he has aimed to
do right, however imperfectly his purposes have been
carried out. It was not in a spirit of boasting or
self-righteousness that the apostle Paul referred so
often to his own upright life and aims. It was not
inconsistent with his deep and permanent conviction
of his own entire destitution of all merit as a ground

of hope, that he referred to his conscientious en-
deavours to live an upright life, or that he commended
his own course as an example to others. Paradoxical
as it may seem, it was the same Paul who said, "I
know that in me (that is, in my flesh) dwelleth no good
thing : O wretched man that I am ! who shall deliver
me from the body of this death ?" "God forbid that
I should glory save in the cross"—who said also, else-
where, "I have lived in all good conscience before God
until this day;" "We have wronged no man, we have
corrupted no man, we have defrauded no man;"
"Brethren, be followers together of me, and mark
them which walk so as ye have us for an ensample;"
"Ye know after what manner I have been with you
at all seasons, serving the Lord with all humility of
mind and with many tears. I have kept back nothing
that was profitable unto you, and have taught you
publicly and from house to house. I have not
shunned to declare unto you all the counsel of God.
I have coveted no man's silver, or gold, or apparel;"
and who said of himself when he was about to die,
"I have fought a good fight ; I have kept the faith."
Imperfect as the life of any man may have been, and
pained as he may be in view of its short-comings and
failures, yet he may have cheerful recollections, and
may find happiness in reflecting that he has been
engaged in a righteous cause, and that his aim has been

to promote the welfare, temporal and eternal, of his fellow-men.

As a man stands on the verge of the grave, and looks out on the eternal world now *very near*, it will not grieve him to reflect that he has sincerely endeavoured to live a life of virtue, temperance, justice, and charity; that he has by example and by precept, commended to the world a way of living which would be for the good of all; that he has endeavoured to save men from ruin by bringing before their minds the way of salvation, and by warning the sinner of his danger; that he has sought to acquaint the world with the doctrine of the immortality of the soul, and the doctrine of the atonement for sin, and the doctrine of the resurrection of the dead,—and to inspire men with the hope of a better life; that he has sought to make all men better, purer, happier, and to diffuse abroad over all lands, faith in a pure religion. It will be a consolation to him then to reflect that he has *not* sought to destroy the faith of men in God, in the Saviour, in the Bible, in the immortality of the soul, in the future state; that he has done nothing to counteract the efforts of parents to train up their children in the ways of virtue, temperance, and pure religion; that he has endeavoured to persuade men to love their country, to love their race, and to strive to promote the welfare of the whole world, irrespective of the limits of rank, of complexion, or of geographical boundaries.

There are two kinds of reflection which men have when they come to review their lives in the prospect of the eternal world. The one arises from the conviction of their own minds that their lives have been wasted; that they have prostituted their talents for purposes of evil; that they have lived to counteract the efforts of the friends of virtue and religion, and to spread error and delusion over the world; that they have, by their writings or their lives, unsettled the faith of men in God, in the Bible, in the Saviour, in the hope of a future life; that they have lived to make men sceptics, and to fill the world with doubt and despair. The other arises from the consciousness, that, however imperfect they may have been, they have sought to make men better, purer, happier; to hold before the guilty and dying the truth that there is a God and a Saviour; to show to all that there is something worth living for; to light up hope, and peace, and joy, in a dark world of sin and sorrow.

I urge now, in conclusion, this fact—that solemn reflections on the past must occur when one reaches the closing scene of life, and that a man will then wish to find evidence that he has so lived as not to lead others astray from the path of virtue, or to weaken their faith in God, or to destroy their hope of a better life,—as a motive addressed to the young, and to all classes of persons, for lending their names and their influence to the cause of virtue, of temperance, of truth, of pure religion. No man regrets such a course when he comes to die.

My life has been a favoured life. I know not that I have an enemy on the earth—that there is one human being who wishes me ill. I am certain that no wrong has been done to me, the recollection of which I desire to cherish, or which it is not easy to forgive.

> "So glide my life away! And so, at last,
>   My share of duties decently fulfilled,
>   May some disease, not tardy to perform
>   Its destined office, yet with gentle stroke,
>   Dismiss me weary to a safe retreat
>   Beneath the turf that I have often trod."

APPENDIX.

———◆———

I. *THE FUNERAL SERVICES.*

II. *THE ACTION OF THE CONGREGATION.*

III. *THE ACTION OF THE SESSION.*

IV. *THE MEMORIAL SERMON.*

I.

THE FUNERAL SERVICES.

———◦◦◦———

THE wish expressed by Mr. Barnes, at the close of the foregoing discourse, was literally realized. "His death," writes his widow, "was sudden and entirely unexpected. His health, with the exception of his eyesight, seemed to be perfect,— mind and body active and full of energy. The day he died, he spent the morning in the city, dined with us cheerfully as usual, and afterwards walked with my daughter about a mile and a quarter into the country, to visit some friends in deep affliction. They reached the house, and he conversed for a few minutes, when he threw back his head, breathed rather heavily, and before the physician, who was immediately summoned, could arrive, he had passed away. In an instant, as it seemed, without pain or any consciousness of entering the 'dark valley,' he was with his Saviour."

In pursuance of arrangements previously made, the Session and Trustees of the First Church, with the family and immediate friends of Mr. BARNES, met shortly before noon, Wednesday, December 28th, 1870, at his residence, where an opportunity was afforded those who wished it to take a last look at the remains.

Prayer was offered by Rev. ROBERT ADAIR, D.D. At noon the body was placed in the hearse, and, accompanied by those in attendance, conveyed to the church in Washington Square. Three members of the Session and three Trustees acted as carriers.

On arriving at the church, the procession was joined by the officiating Clergy, and by the following gentlemen, who acted as Pall Bearers :—

Rev. HENRY J. MORTON, D.D., of St. James's Protestant Episcopal Church, Philadelphia.—Rev. C. H. PAYNE, D.D., of the Methodist Episcopal Church, Philadelphia.—Rev. JAMES CROWELL, D.D., of the Woodlands Presbyterian Church, Philadelphia.—Rev. WM. P. BREED, D.D., of the West Spruce Street Presbyterian Church.— Rev. EDGAR M. LEVY, D.D., of the Baptist Church, West Philadelphia.—Rev. T. W. J. WYLIE, D.D., of the Reformed Presbyterian Church, Philadelphia.—Rev. Z. M. HUMPHREY, D.D., of Calvary Presbyterian Church.—Hon. WILLIAM STRONG, LL.D., Associate Justice of the Supreme Court United States and Elder in Calvary Presbyterian Church.—Hon. GEORGE SHARSWOOD, LL.D., Associate Justice of the Supreme Court of Pennsylvania and Elder in Penn Square Presbyterian Church.—Hon. JOSEPH ALLISON, Presiding Judge Court of Common Pleas, Philadelphia, and Elder in the West Walnut Street Presbyterian Church.—JOHN NEILL, M.D., Physician of the family.— J. MARSHALL PAUL, M.D., Elder of Belvidere Church.

Delegates were present from the American Philosophical Society; the Managers of the House of Refuge; the Pennsylvania Bible Society; and the Trustees of the University of Pennsylvania. A large number of clergymen of various denominations were also in attendance. The pulpit and front of the galleries were draped in black.

After a Chant, "Blessed are the dead," (Rev. xiv. 13,) the invocation-prayer was offered by the Rev. HERRICK JOHNSON, D.D.

Appropriate selections from the Word of God were then read by the Rev. ALEXANDER REED, D.D. ; followed by the Hymn, " Why do we mourn departing friends?"

The Rev. THOMAS H. SKINNER, D.D., delivered an address, in which he spoke of the departed as "a man of God pre-eminently gifted ; one who had an analytical, a logical, a pre-eminently philological mind ; one in whom there was matter for praise—for glorying ; yet the praise did not belong to him, but to God in him ; and if Mr. Barnes could be present that day and hear a word, the meaning of which should be glory to him originally, he would not concur in that ascription. No man excelled him, so far as I know, in the sense of obligation to God for the different endowments he possessed. The senti-ment of the Apostle was ever his own, 'Who maketh thee to differ from another? And what hast thou that thou hast not received?' . . . His life had been full of Divine favour. . . . And oh, what occasion there was to glorify God, on account of the manner of his death ! We bleed to lose such a man, but the manner of his death fills us with delight, with joy. I have not been able, brethren, to unite in the prayer to be delivered from sudden death. Unless you mean by ' sudden' unprepared, I can-not join in that prayer. But if I am ready to die, oh, give me such a death as that which God in His love and mercy gave to my beloved brother Barnes." . . . .

The Rev. WILLIAM BACON STEVENS, D.D., Bishop of the Protestant Episcopal Church, next spoke, and he claimed Mr. Barnes as belonging to all Christendom. " True greatness consists in doing a great work from a great motive, and for a great end. He did a great work ; not merely in this pulpit, which he occupied so many years ;

not merely in this community, where his name was a tower of strength and of honour,—but in the quiet of that study and in the early morning hours, when night was still lingering over the city, he wrote out those works which have been scattered broadcast over the Christian world, and which have done as much, perhaps, to mould the Christian thought and fortify the Christian heart as anything that has emanated from man for the last century. And it is a work that is still going on. He being dead, yet speaketh, and the hundreds of thousands of volumes that are scattered through a hundred thousand families here and abroad, all these are still speaking, and they will speak as long as there is a Christian literature to give its utterance to Christian minds. . . . What a great thing did he accomplish by this work! What a difference there is between the state of Biblical education this day and what it was when he first began to write this series of books in yonder study! And to whom are we more indebted for this great advance in Biblical exegetical science than we are to the dear brother whose body lies before us? and oh, if God honours His Holy Word as He has honoured it, by making it, as it were, the great light in the moral firmament, truly Albert Barnes did a great thing when he sought to turn the eyes of men to that light, that in that light they might find light, and thus, as children of the light and of the day, walk on in that path of light which shineth more and more unto the perfect day. . . . . When I heard of his sudden death, I felt my heart leap up almost with gladness, that one who had lived among us so apparently strong,— who had been the cynosure of so many eyes,—around whom had clustered so many affections,—and who received wherever he went the tribute of reverence and respect, had been taken up almost as Elijah was, and that we could almost see the chariot of fire and the horses of fire that separated this Elijah, as he went up, from our young Elisha who remains behind. We bless God for such a death; it was, indeed, a translation, for the light of his life set in death—

> 'As sets the morning star,
> Which goes not down behind the darkened west,
> Nor hides obscured 'midst tempests of the sky,
> But *melts away into the light of heaven.*'"

The third address was delivered by the Rev. JOHN CHAMBERS, who forty years ago, had conducted the preliminary services, when ALBERT BARNES delivered his first sermon to the congregation who had called him to fill the place of one the brightest lights of the American pulpit. "It would be folly in me," he said "in a community like this, to attempt an eulogy upon the character of the Rev. Albert Barnes. He is above all human eulogy. His whole life, ever since he first stepped into this house of God, has been a sublime commentary upon the grace of God, which converts the heart. No man, in the past or present, in this city ever maintained a purer life. He was the most unpretentious of men—among the most gentle, at the same time among the most manly of men. He loved the truth; he stood by it with the firmness of a rock. No power or influence on earth could have induced him to compromise it. If ever a man walked upon a pathway of righteousness, luminous as a sunbeam, my brother and friend walked upon that pathway, everywhere exemplifying the beauties and the glories of a regenerated nature. I have said it to myself, and this morning in the ear of a brother minister, that, if every man who claimed to be a minister of Jesus Christ since the days of the Apostles had loved Christ, lived Christ, and preached

Christ as Albert Barnes did, and left such a legacy of Christian piety and ministerial fidelity as he has left, all the world, to-day, would be *almost*, if not entirely, under the baptism of the Holy Ghost.   His life was literally devoted to his Master's cause.   He loved to preach.   More than once I have heard him say : ' The courtesies of life induce me to ask my brethren to fill my pulpit—my choice is never to sit idle.'   To the very end of life he manifested the same attachment to the principles of the Gospel.   To-day we are called upon to mourn the loss of one of the mightiest of men in the cause of the Son of God.   He has left to this community, he has left to this congregation, he has left to the cause of the Son of God a legacy that will live till time ends." . . . .

Another Hymn was sung :—

Asleep in Jesus ! blessed sleep,
From which none ever waked to weep !
A calm and undisturbed repose,
Unbroken by the last of foes.

Asleep in Jesus ! Oh ! how sweet,
To be for such a slumber meet !
With holy confidence to sing,
That death has lost his venomed sting.

Asleep in Jesus ! peaceful rest,
Whose waking is supremely blest !
No fear, no woe, shall dim that hour
Which manifests the Saviour's power.

Asleep in Jesus ! Oh ! for me
May such a blissful refuge be !
Securely shall my ashes lie,
And wait the summons from on high.

An Address by the Rev. HERRICK JOHNSON, D.D., gave the following interesting details :—

"It is not for me to protract this service by further or more elaborate eulogy. I trust the privilege will be mine ere long to speak at length, and with some fulness, of the character and life of him whom we mourn to-day. I would detain you now only with a few words of reminiscence. When I came to stand in his place, to break the bread of life where he so faithfully had served his Master for well-nigh half a century, he gave me the welcome and the kiss of a father; and from that hour to the hour of his death, never, by a word or a deed or a look, did he intimate to me in any way that I was not honoured with his confidence, his love, and his benediction, and I came to love him as a son.

"I remember his standing in this place, a little more than two years ago, to give the accustomed pastoral charge to me, by the appointment of the Presbytery and by the request of his dear flock. I recalled the words of that charge when I heard of his sudden departure; and turning to it to-day, I found there an eulogy from his own lips upon another, that seems the very truest and most fitting that could be pronounced in this presence to-day upon himself. They were words descriptive of the man who thirty-eight years before, in this same pulpit, had given the pastoral charge to ALBERT BARNES. In that description Mr. Barnes most beautifully and appropriately and truthfully described himself, although he had no thought then that he was portraying his own character in the portraiture he drew of another. He said of that memorable man, who gave him his charge, who is still living, and who has stood in our presence to-day, to glorify God in the life and character of the deceased : 'A most venerable and lovely man; a man without guile ; a man, though over seventy, with intellect as clear, as bright, as logical, as in his most vigorous days ; a man of most pure spirit, to be loved by whom is an honour of the highest kind ; a man still laborious in the Master's cause, and bringing forth fruit in old age ; who shows by his daily life how lovely Christian piety is when one has lived all his days near to God, and how it grows and brightens as its possessor stands on the verge of heaven, and the light of the eternal throne seems to beam upon him.' Did not Mr. Barnes so stand last Saturday guileless in character, ripened into a golden completeness, on the very verge of heaven, the light from the eternal throne beaming upon him?

" I remember how, three weeks ago last Sabbath, we came together in this house of God; and he, as was his wont on such occasions, came with us to celebrate what has proved to be his last Sacramental Supper. This First Church will never forget that precious season. Our banqueting house was like an outer court of heaven, and the words of Mr. Barnes were prophetic of what has now come in the providence of God. He then, for the first time since I came into this church as its pastor, reviewed the history of his ministry ; spoke tenderly of the dear departed who had been called of God, one by one, and taken away,—and of the very few that still lingered upon the shores of time, who were here to welcome him to this pastorate forty years ago. There we sat and wept and talked and supped together, he and his dear Lord and his beloved people. He said it might be the last time that he would ever break bread at that table. There before us was the symbol of the broken body of his dear Lord. We little thought, as he gave it to us, with words of unusual tenderness, that here, to-day, at the same altar his own body would lie.

"I recall the sermon he preached one week ago last Sabbath morning—the last sermon he ever preached on earth. He stood in this sacred desk, and, with unusual vitality, gave his last message to the people of his charge, setting forth clearly and fully and exhaustively the plan of redemption through Jesus Christ, taking for his text these memorable words—words which I believe he might have chosen if he could have known that it was his last message: 'Mercy and truth are met together, righteousness and peace have kissed each other.'

"I recall his last evening—the last evening he ever spent on earth, when a few of his friends were with him, how cheerful, how hopeful, how vigorous, how full of energy he was. He then expressed the oft-repeated wish that he might live a thousand years. God granted his wish, for he is not dead; he did not consciously die. What to us was death, was to him transition. God shielded him from the gloom and the sorrow and the night of death. Angels from the Presence came through the golden gates of the city of God, and with unseen hands they opened wide the doors of the gates of death, swinging them back noiselessly on their hinges; then they came this side of where death's shadows fall, and canopying this dear man of God about with their golden wings, and lighting him about with their reflected glory, they so bore him into and out of the valley of shadows that he never knew he was passing through. There was no darkness, no night. At eventide it was light. He was borne as on a chariot of angelic golden wings to heaven. Fitting close of such a life. Well done, good and faithful servant; thou hast entered into the joy of thy Lord !"

Prayer having been offered by the Rev. Daniel March,

D.D.,—thanking God, as the "Supreme Giver of every good and perfect gift, for the wonderful power that was given to His servant, to draw the minds of millions to the study of the Scriptures; for the great industry and conscientiousness with which he used that sacred talent; for the words of instruction which he was permitted to send out into all the earth; for the meekness and lowliness with which he bore his great faculties in the service of God; for the blamelessness and purity with which he held his holy office as the minister of Christ; for the uprightness and integrity with which he fulfilled his obligations to his fellow-men; for the sympathy and brotherly kindness with which he shared his brethren's burdens and helped them in their work; for his great skill and candour in removing the difficulties which burden and embarrass the doubting mind; for the clearness and simplicity with which he unfolded the dark ways of Providence and the deep things of the Word; for his earnest sympathy with the suffering; for his brave and faithful words in behalf of the poor and oppressed; for his quick and keen sensibility to the demands of truth and justice and honour; for the sincerity and manliness with which he gave himself for the defence of every good and holy cause; for the light and hope which he was permitted to kindle in so many homes, in so many hearts; for the good name which he acquired as a minister and as a man; for the unsullied reputation, with which he stood forth before the world, as the representative of pure and undefiled religion in the city of his home and in the land of his birth;"—and commending to the Divine Comforter, whose mercies can never fail, the widow and the children in their bereavement, the church to which for many years he had ministered, the successor called to fill his place, and all who had borne the responsibilities of the sacred office as fellow-labourers with the deceased,—the Benediction (Heb. xiii. 20, 21) was pronounced by the Rev. T. H. SKINNER, D.D.

At the close of the services the body was carried to the hearse, and taken to North Laurel Hill Cemetery, attended by members of the family, the Session and Trustees of the Church, and many friends.

The body was then committed to the dust, and the last rites of the living paid to the beloved dead.

The service at the grave consisted of brief selections from the Scripture,—prayer,—and the Apostolic Benediction, by the Rev. HERRICK JOHNSON, D.D.

II.

THE ACTION OF THE CONGREGATION.

A T a Congregational Meeting held Wednesday, December 28th, 1870, the following preamble and resolutions were unanimously adopted :

"WHEREAS we have this day interred the mortal remains of our beloved Pastor Emeritus, the REVEREND ALBERT BARNES, who has been so suddenly called to be with his Redeemer in his eternal home ; therefore,

"*Resolved*, That we his people will ever cherish a most thankful remembrance of his many years of faithful and blessed ministry with us ; of his precious teachings, fraught with the wisdom that comes from above ; of the bright example of his holy life and of his kindly and loving converse with us. We revere his pure and unstained character, and rejoice to have been united by so many ties with one so lovely in all the associations of life, and of such widely extended usefulness in the kingdom of our Lord.

"We would be submissive to the Divine decree ; we acknowledge that the Judge of all the earth does that which is right ; and while we sympathize with the bereaved family and weep with those who weep, we would look up through our tears unto Him who not only has borne our griefs and carried our sorrows, but has abolished death and brought immortality to light."

III.

THE ACTION OF THE SESSION.

———◦◦◦———

AT a Special Meeting of the Session of the First Presbyterian Church held on Saturday evening, December 31st, 1870, the following minute was adopted, ordered to be entered on the minutes of the Session, and a copy sent to the family of the deceased :—

" After forty years of almost uninterrupted ministerial and pastoral labour, in connection with this church, it has pleased God, who called our beloved pastor into the ministry, to call him away from it. While fruitful still in good works, his ardour unabated, his intellect clear and his form erect, he was summoned to his rest. He came to the grave 'in a full age, like as a shock of corn cometh in in his season.' He walked with God, and he was not, for God took him.

" We desire to put on record, as a Session, our deep sense of personal and official bereavement. We sorrow most of all that we shall see his face no more. We bow in tears before the Providence that has ended the association of so many precious years.

" But, for the loving fellowship of all these years, we thank God to-day.

" For all that ALBERT BARNES has been to his country and to the world, we thank God.

"For his pulpit efficiency, and for his pastoral fidelity, we thank God.

"For his personal courtesy, for his rare conscientiousness in the discharge of all the duties of his sacred office, for his guileless character, ripening ever to a beautiful and golden completeness during the forty years of his pastorate of our beloved Church, we thank God.

"For all that he has been to us and to our children, for his instructions in righteousness, for his faithful rebukes, for his loving counsels, and for his precious prevailing prayers, we thank God.

"As a preacher of the Word, we bear record that he never broke faith with the truth.

"As a pastor, he won his way into our homes and hearts, and ever had welcome there, walking in the midst of us, loved and honoured and trusted.

"As a Moderator and member of the Session, he took sweet counsel with us; and we make glad and grateful mention of his unvarying urbanity and considerate deferential regard during all the years of our official intercourse, as we deliberated together, and watched and prayed over this dear flock of God.

"In memory of his life and death, in gratitude for his word and work, stimulated by his example, and impressed by the startling suddenness of the Providence which has terminated his work on earth, we would here re-consecrate ourselves to the Master he so loved to follow, and give to the Church of his labours and prayers and tears, more fully and faithfully than ever, our energies and our hearts."

IV.

THE MEMORIAL SERMON

PREACHED BY THE

REV. HERRICK JOHNSON, D.D.,

IN THE FIRST PRESBYTERIAN CHURCH, PHILADELPHIA,

January 22, 1871.

— -•◦•- —

"The steps of a good man are ordered by the Lord ; and he delighteth
in his way."—*Psalm* xxxvii. 23.

— -•◦•- —

WITHOUT Divine permission, not a sparrow falls to the ground. The fowls of the air sow not, reap not, gather not into barns, yet the Heavenly Father feedeth them. That arrow, shot from a bow, "drawn at a venture," took no chance flight, but was winged of the invisible God to the smiting of a king between the joints of the harness. The clouds, the winds, the lightnings, are God's obedient and swift messengers. He appointeth the stars their courses. He guides Arcturus with his sons. And amidst the higher orders of creation, by living intelligences, God's purposes and appointments are all truly fulfilled. He doeth according to His will in the armies of heaven, and among the inhabitants of the earth. The way of man is not in himself. It is not in man that walketh to direct his steps. The king's heart is in the hand of the Lord, as the rivers of water; He turneth it whithersoever He will. In Him we live, and move, and have our being. Of Him, and through Him, and to Him, are all things: to whom be glory for ever.

Nothing, therefore, in this world, or any world, is outside God's providential government. It is true of man, whether good or bad, that his steps are ordered by the Lord. And thus the statement of the text stands in the original. It is in form a general proposition. From Jehovah, by Jehovah's direction, the steps of a man have been settled; his course of life has been fixed. But the context clearly demands a specific application of this truth to the righteous. It is of the good, the upright, the righteous man, in contrast with the wicked, that the Psalmist is speaking. It is one in whose way God takes *pleasure.* Hence our translators have supplied the word "good;" and the passage reads, "The steps of a good man are ordered by the Lord, and He delighteth in his way." They are so ordered in a sense in which the steps of a wicked man are not ordered. Both alike are included in God's providential government. Both alike come under His all-comprehensive and predetermined plan. To Him there are no unexpected revolutions, no unforeseen contingencies, no startling and sudden surprises along the courses of history. The countless determinations of man's free will are as determinate in the mind of God, as the revolutions of His obedient stars. But the steps of the wicked are not established as the steps of the righteous are. In the one case God's agency is largely permissive; in the other it is efficient. In the one case it is with condemnation, in the other with approval. God tempts no man to evil; but He does tempt man to good. He directly influences in the right course. He withholds His influence in the wrong course. His ordering of the steps of a good man is more as a father. It is mingled with tenderest love and care. "He knows the way of the righteous"—knows to approve it and take pleasure in it. God "delighteth in his way. Though he fall, he shall not be utterly cast down, for the Lord upholdeth him with His hand. Mark the perfect man, and behold the upright: for the end of that man is peace."

This truth and these words have seldom had so fit an illustration as in the life of ALBERT BARNES. That his were the steps of a good man, there is no one now to question. That they were ordered of the Lord, we had this clear and full acknowledgment from his own lips at threescore and ten: "I have carried out none of the purposes of my early years. I have failed in those things which I had designed, and which I hoped to accomplish. I have done what I never purposed or expected to do. I have known what it was to weep at discouragements. I have been led along contrary to my early anticipations. I can now see, I think, that while I have been conscious of entire freedom in all that I have done, yet my whole life has been under the absolute control of a higher power, and there has been a will and plan in regard to my life which was not my own. Even my most voluntary acts I can see have been subservient to that higher plan, and what I have done has been done as if I had no agency in the matter." Thus unqualifiedly did this good man admit

"There's a divinity that shapes our ends,
Rough-hew them how we will."

But beyond this, into the shaping of *his* ends, into the ordering of *his* steps, there entered elements of Divine and parental love and care. It was something more than an overruling Providence that gave direction to his life. It was an interested and approving Providence. That God delighted in his way is the demanded inference from all Scripture, is proved from the beneficent fruit of his life, is the spontaneous and universal testimony of Christendom. He had occasion to weep at discouragements, indeed; he was sometimes disappointed: he knew the bitterness of a wounded spirit; there were painful months and stormy years in his three-score years and ten; but he was never utterly cast down, for the Lord upheld him. His early trials purified the gold of his Christian character. He was uplifted into the region of great calm. He did a grand work for God, and his end was "peace."

Born at Rome, in the State of New York, December 1, 1798, "blessed with virtuous and industrious parents," he entered at an early age upon the occupation of his father as a tanner; but was turned aside from this by the suggestion of a country schoolmaster, and persuaded to pursue at Fairfield Academy, in the town of Fairfield, a course of studies preparatory to the profession of law. He entered the senior class of Hamilton College in the fall of 1819. There he was "born again"—born to God, and at the age of manhood he first began to live. Graduated in 1820, and consecrated now to the work of the ministry, he entered the Theological Seminary at Princeton, N.J.; pursued the regular course of study: was licensed to preach the gospel April 23, 1823, by the Presbytery of New Brunswick; remained one year at Princeton as a resident licentiate; and was ordained and installed as pastor of the Presbyterian Church in Morristown, N.J., by the Presbytery of Elizabethtown, Feb. 8, 1825. After a pastorate of nearly five years he was called to the pastoral charge of the First Presbyterian Church of Philadelphia, and installed by the Presbytery of Philadelphia, June 25, 1830. Here for thirty-seven years he discharged his official duties, resigning his charge November 18, 1867, when he was unanimously elected *Pastor emeritus.* He died December 24, 1870.

Those two records—born, December 1, 1798, died December 24, 1870—mark the limits of a life that has few parallels for simplicity, dignity, gentleness, truthfulness, usefulness, guilelessness, devotion to duty, and walk with God.

There was nothing in the opening years of Mr. Barnes's life of special moment. But he was thought by one who had something to do with his early development, to give promise of more than ordinary efficiency. And by this teacher, he and a young friend and school-mate were induced, with the somewhat reluctant consent of their parents, to enter upon a preparation for the legal profession. His classmate entered that profession, rose to eminence in it, and ultimately occupied the highest judicial position in his native State. He himself was led subsequently to make choice of a different profession. He began life a sceptic in religion. Up to the age of nineteen he had no belief in the Bible as a revelation from God. It was doubtless this early intellectual scepticism which gave him ever afterwards the pre-eminent characteristic of clearness in perceiving, and of fairness in stating, the difficulties and objections of the disbeliever. It was doubtless this, also, that led to his unusual caution in admitting a statement to his belief, or a person to his confidence, until the statement or the person was proved to be worthy of his trust. He was accustomed to say that doubts and difficulties born of his own questioning and sceptical heart, had seemed to him to be of far greater force and magnitude than any he had ever seen suggested by rationalism and infidelity. An article in the Edinburgh *Encyclopædia,* by Dr. Chalmers, entitled "Christianity," first commanded his assent to the truth and Divine origin of the Christian religion. But he resolved to yield to its claims no farther than thenceforward to keep aloof from its active opposers, and to lead a strictly moral life. This intellectual change was followed a year later by a deeper and more radical change, wrought not by the logic of man, but by the power of God. The instrumentality was a classmate in college, fresh from the joy of recent espousals with Jesus, whose simple statement of his own personal experience without any direct appeal whatever, went to the young moralist's heart, and was the means, under God, of his conversion. Thus, by so slight an incident, were set in entirely new channels the currents of a life; and they have gone the wide world over, making the wilderness glad for them, and causing many a moral desert-place to rejoice and blossom. Mr. Barnes always spoke of this as the great change that materially affected all his plans in this life, and which he anticipated and hoped would affect his condition for ever. It gave to the world "The People's Commentator." It gave to the Church one of the purest and truest of her living epistles. It gave to the ministry as faithful a herald as ever declared the counsel of God. How little that new-born disciple knew what he was doing for Jesus, by telling what Jesus had done for him! How signal the illustration that "weak things" in human estimation, often have almightiness for their ally in God's plan!

At the very gateway of his new life, Mr. Barnes abandoned his purpose of entering the legal profession, and consecrated himself to the work of the ministry. At the theological seminary he was a diligent and faithful student. Writing from there to a friend and former companion, near the close of the first year of his seminary life, April 24, 1821, he said with an unaffected humility and a conscious unworthiness that characterized him through all his subsequent successes, "The little anxiety I feel for the souls of my fellow-men, the little zeal for my Master's glory, and the pride and corruption of my own heart, often make me tremble when I look forward to the holy ministry, and fear that I am rushing uncalled into the harvest of the Lord."

Finishing his course at Princeton, and perfecting himself for his work by an added year of study, he entered on his first responsible charge as pastor of the Presbyterian Church at Morristown. He went to this field of labour from the seminary, indorsed by his professors as a man of humble piety, spiritual and earnest, irrepressible in desire, and of indomitable perseverance—one of the most promising of the alumni. He was thoroughly examined by the Presbytery, and ordained and installed with great unanimity. Here he organized and held Bible classes in the school-houses of the outlying districts of his parish. Here he formed or confirmed those exact habits and methods which were of such incalculable advantage to him in the prosecution of his life-work. Whatever the weather, the young and earnest pastor was always in his seat promptly at the appointed hour, Bible and note-book in hand. Here, too, he was struck with the need of a plain and simple commentary on the Gospels, which could be put into the hands of teachers and which would furnish an easy explanation of the meaning of the sacred writers. The Sabbath-school was then assuming vast importance as an institution preeminently calculated to deepen the impression of scriptural truth, and to fix it permanently in the minds of the young. Impressed with the importance of just views of interpretation, and aiming only to be instrumental in extending such views, and in promoting practical piety and the knowledge of the word of God among the youth of this country, he at once entered upon those Scripture studies, the fruits of which were subsequently given in " Notes Explanatory and Practical on the Gospels: Designed for Sunday-school Teachers and Bible Classes." He little dreamed, then, that the purpose thus formed, and upon the prosecution of which he thus early entered, would make his name a household word wherever the English tongue is spoken. He had no thought in the unambitious effort to give simply the results of the critical study of the Gospels, and (by avoiding all abstruse and scholastic discussion) to afford a useful interpreter to the young and the unlearned, that he was to place himself foremost among Bible commentators as to the number of his readers, and to go around the world like the beautiful feet of morning, publishing in varied languages his exposition of the word and work of Christ. But thus were the steps of this good man ordered by the Lord.

It was during his pastorate at Morristown also, that he took bold and decided ground in favour of the cause of temperance. The great work of the temperance reformation commenced about the time he entered his public ministry. Personally and officially he sprang to the advocacy of its great leading principle,—entire abstinence from all intoxicating beverages. And to the day of his death he remained true to it.

Alcoholic beverages were extensively manufactured and sold in the region of country where he first ministered, and the usual drinking customs prevailed in the community. I have heard him, in a spirit of pleasantry, allude to the fact that when he began his ministry there were nineteen distilleries under his pastoral charge, and twenty places within the limits of his parish where liquor was sold. To his lasting honour, and to the praise of God for His signal blessing on signal ministerial fidelity, let it be recorded that, by reason of this young pastor's plain, earnest, and successive appeals to the reason, the conscience, and the heart of his people, in eighteen out of the twenty places where intoxicating drinks were sold the traffic was soon abandoned, and in seventeen out of nineteen of those places where the poison was manufactured the fires went out to be rekindled no more. What Mr. Barnes understood to be the truth of God on this subject, and which he fearlessly preached, he nevertheless so presented as to win his hearers to its approval, although it demanded great pecuniary sacrifices and compelled a complete revolution in some of the most cherished and most fortified habits of social life. Thirty years afterwards, when the barriers that had been raised against intemperance were measurably broken down, —when the flood-gates of this iniquity seemed again to be thrown wide open,—when the voice of warning and entreaty had almost died away, and the press was silent and other pulpits were dumb, he dared be singular in refusing to break faith with his convictions and to shrink from their avowal; and at the age of three-score, standing in this pulpit, he said, after a reference to his first official and successful advocacy of the cause,—" I have maintained publicly the same principles since. I have defended the cause of temperance in every way in my power. I have advocated the principle of total abstinence from all that can intoxicate; I have vindicated the use of ' the pledge;' I have argued against those laws which contemplate the *licensing* of that which is admitted to be an evil; I have exhorted the Church to set an example of total abstinence; I have endeavoured to show that the manufacture and sale of ardent spirits for drinking purposes can be reconciled neither with the principles of sound morality nor religion; I have defended the propriety of a law which would wholly prohibit the sale of alcoholic drinks except for purposes of medicine and manufactures. I have endeavoured to show you, that as you would not suffer a powder manufactory to be set up in Washington Square; as you would not allow a cargo of damaged hides to be landed at your wharves; as you would not permit a vessel from an infected region to come into port, so the true and the safe principle would be to exclude and prohibit for ever that which spreads woe, poverty, disease, crime, pollution, and death; that a community is bound to protect itself; and that no class of men, for private gain, can have a right to scatter death and ruin around the land."*

He adhered unswervingly to these principles, and

* 'Life at Threescore,' pp. 36, 37.

publicly advocated them on all suitable occasions till he died. After a long and useful life he bore unequivocal testimony to the *gain* which came to him, personally and officially, from the adoption of the principles of total abstinence. He said: "I cannot believe that I should have been more useful to any class of men by adopting a different course. I am certain that I should have been less useful to many; that many to whom I would have been glad to be useful would have been pained if I had pursued a different course, and would have made it an objection against the Gospel which I could not readily have met."* Who does not feel that these words are solemnly true? Would to God the testimony of the life of Albert Barnes might lead all who ponder them to the belief he so firmly cherished from his young manhood to his grave, that the only safe and correct principle for an individual, if he would promote his health, his prosperity, his reputation, his usefulness here, and his salvation in the world to come, is that of total abstinence.

During Mr. Barnes's first pastorate, and for the better part of his subsequent life, there was another social evil in the land, of which he was just as courageous and earnest, and consistent and persistent an opposer as he was of intemperance. He believed always in the brotherhood of our common humanity. He was early persuaded of the guilt and the crime

* 'Life at Threescore,' p. 33.

of human bondage. His first critical study of the New Testament, there in the quiet of his home at Morristown, led him to feel and to say that the Gospel was an epistle of deliverance to the captives; that to give liberty to the slave, and restore him to freedom, was to confer the highest benefit and impart the richest favour; and that by the freedom of the truth all prison doors would finally be opened, and all chains of slavery broken. From that time onward he never hesitated, from the pulpit and by the press, in the clearest and most unmistakable terms to express his convictions on the evils, the crimes, the wrongs of slavery. He regarded the system of human bondage, to use his own language, "as opposed to the spirit of religion, destructive of the welfare of society, a violation of human rights, and contrary to the will of God." He was no enthusiast or fanatic in this matter. He was not in anything. Behind his boldest, and freest, and most radical utterances there was no passionate excess of feeling—only the calm, sober conviction of a truth-loving, earnest, conscientious man of God; and to give that conviction embodiment in speech on fit occasion, at whatever risk and at whatever cost, was as much a matter of course with him as to eat his daily bread.

I am assured he never attended an anti-slavery convention in his life. He was never a member of an anti-slavery society. He never travelled out of his appointed path to condemn slavery. It was in the direct channels of his influence that he opposed the institution. Yet he found appropriate occasion and felt called of God on this subject more often than on any other except temperance, apart from the regular topics of preaching, to express his convictions. And this he did, according to his own testimony, when for many years he stood almost alone on the subject in the ministry of this city. He did it in face of much opposition. He did it in peril of his place among his people. When there was odium attached to it, and when a strong public and even Christian sentiment set sweepingly against it, and when the authorities of the city were opposed to such freedom of discussion,—he did it then. When the Mayor, and the police, and the firemen, and the citizens generally, looked on calmly, if not exultingly, while the Pennsylvania Hall, devoted to the free discussion of this subject as well as others, was fired by a mob, and was burned to the ground, and when it seemed necessary that some public voice should be lifted up in favour of the right of free discussion, and in behalf of the oppressed and the wronged in our land, this brave spirit came into this pulpit the next Sabbath, and did it then. He preached a sermon on "The supremacy of the laws," in which he aimed to make clear and to emphasize the peril and the guilt of suffering the laws to be prostrated by a mob. He did it notably again, when in January, 1861, in the course of a regular exposition of the Psalms, he came to the fifty-second, and delivered a discourse on Doeg, the Edomite, or the Informer; wherein he declared that if a man should come to him as a fugitive from oppression anywhere, he would treat him precisely as he would desire that his own son should be treated in a similar case; and the man should find in him a helper and a sympathizing friend, rather than a mean informer.

Not that he would oppose law. Not that he ever lent countenance to any agency designed to induce a slave to escape from his master. He never uttered a word, in public or in private, in favour of any illegal interference with the institution, where it existed. What he did, and all that he did, beyond endeavouring to secure a constitutional change of the laws, was done as a preacher and a commentator by a candid and thoughtful exposition of the Word of God in its application to the duties and the rights of man. In his pulpit and in his Notes he never sought popularity by silence. Turn to any page of his Commentary where there is a passage regarded as bearing upon the subject of slavery, and there it will be seen that he ever consistently entered a calm, vigorous, solemn, Christian protest against this (at that time) strongly buttressed and gospel-defended, but, in his judgment, most abominable institutional iniquity. He wrote and published a book as the result of his Biblical study in this direction, entitled,

"An Inquiry into the Scriptural View of Slavery," which has been characterized as a book of calm and gentle words, but very hard arguments.

During the last eventful years of his life, he saw what he had never dared to hope he would be privileged with seeing in this mortal life—America without a slave! He thanked God that he could die closing his eyes on a land where every man could look into the face of every other and say, "I, too, am free!" In his advanced years he entered heartily into the work of educating and elevating the long-enthralled race, of which his official and efficient connection with Lincoln University bore ample witness.

To the last he was the active and sympathizing friend of the helpless and the unfortunate. Not long after he resigned the pastorate of the First Church, owing to failing sight, and when he was nearly threescore years and ten, he was met by a friend officially connected with the House of Refuge, and the conversation then ensuing resulted in his accepting a proposition to become a member of the board of managers of that institution. He entered at once upon the discharge of his duties, and immediately took his place on some of the most laborious committees, and those which brought him directly in contact with six hundred wayward and neglected children, gathered within the walls of the House of Refuge. He voluntarily offered his services to officiate statedly in the Sabbath services of the chapels of the Refuge; and for some time prior to his death he preached on the third Sabbath of each month to the children of the coloured department, and on the fourth Sabbath of each month to the children of the white department. No circumstances that he could control were allowed to interfere with these self-imposed duties; and his interest grew and deepened in this new and unusual charge as the months went on. Perhaps no more endearing testimonials of the veneration in which he was held in the institution could be given than those volunteered by both teachers and pupils of the schools, and sent by them to the board of managers, upon their hearing of his sudden death. The teachers say: " His whole heart was engaged in this labour of love; and his winning smile and encouraging word never failed to impart joy and gladness to both teachers and scholars." The boys say, in a testimonial which is the unaided production of one of their own number: " We wish, in an humble and heartfelt manner, to express our sincere regrets for the death of our dear friend and benefactor." And farther on they add: " We do not know as much of his career connected with the community at large as we do concerning him in connection with this institution; but we do know that a kinder and more loving heart, or more generous and sympathizing nature, never has come among us."

The last sermon that he preached on earth was to

the children of the House of Refuge, with these closing words: "Children, I do not expect to live long. When I am dead you will remember what I preached to you." They sat waiting for him the next Sabbath —for him whom they never had waited for before— *but he never came.*

The work, however, to which I have yet scarcely alluded, but which came to be, though wholly without design at first, the principal work of this eminently useful and laborious life, and in which probably more than in any other Mr. Barnes was signally successful, was the preparation of Notes or Commentaries on the Sacred Scriptures. To no one was the final result reached so great an astonishment as to the author himself. For this work, he tells us, he had no special preparation, and it never entered into his early plans or expectations. He began, as we have already seen, with the design of preparing only a few plain and simple *Notes on the Gospels,* and mainly for the benefit of Sunday-school teachers and scholars. He entered upon it at Morristown, and prosecuted it upon his transfer to Philadelphia as a *side work* altogether. He gave the early hours of the morning to this pleasurable occupation. Whatever he accomplished in the way of commentary on the Scriptures is to be traced to the fact of his rising at four in the morning. He resolved to leave this work promptly at nine o'clock every day and turn to his more direct pulpit and pastoral duties; and for more than thirty years, until he laid down his pen at the end of his long task, he kept that resolution. His first venture—Notes on the Gospels—bears date, Philadelphia, August 25, 1832. Committing it to the blessing of the God of the Bible, he gave it to the world with the prayer that it might be one among many instruments of forming correct religious views, and promoting the practical love of God and man, among the youth of this country. By the preparation of these first Notes the steps of this good man were established in that quiet path where he "prevented the dawning of the morning" in communion with God, and in the careful and prayerful study of His holy word. He learned to love those still, studious hours. They became to him among the happiest of his life. He grew there, in that close contact with truth, towards Christ-like completeness, until he mirrored in his life that which had exposition by his pen. Truth, to a degree, with him, like truth, without degree, with Jesus, was *swallowed up of personality.* It came to be the chyle and blood and fibre of his spiritual manhood, until men loved to think of him and speak of him as a man of God, in whom was no guile.

The habit of spending a small portion of each day in annotating the Scriptures grew to be a pleasure and a preference, and he continued it until in 1834 appeared his "Notes Explanatory and Practical on the Acts of the Apostles," and on "The Epistle to the

Romans." One book after another followed, as this man of method persevered year by year in his study of the Word, until, to his own surprise, he found himself at the end of the New Testament. Turning to the Old Testament, he prepared his annotations successively on Isaiah, Job, Daniel, and the Psalms. Meanwhile other works in the line of his ministerial labours were published. His pen was never idle. He lived to see edition after edition of his Commentaries exhausted, until more than half a million of volumes were sold in this country, and perhaps even a greater number in England, Scotland, and Ireland; while translations to a limited extent were made into the languages of France, Wales, India, and China. This remarkable result is the fullest proof that the life-labour of Mr. Barnes met a wide necessity. The man needs no other monument commemorative of his faithful toil. Without any original design on his part, when no eyes were turned to him in expectation of any grand achievement, an over-ruling Providence selected the instrumentality, prompted to the conception of the early task, inspired a love for its enlarging way, guided the steps of the faithful expositor, and led to the completion of a work which, for its extent, fidelity, and beneficent influence, is rarely allotted to man. He ended his exposition of the Book of Psalms, February, 1868, with these memorable words, in reference to his labours as a commentator: "I cannot close this work with-

out emotion. I cannot lay down my pen at the
end of this long task without feeling that with me
the work of life is nearly over. Yet I could close it
at no better place than in finishing the exposition of
this book; and the language with which the Book
of Psalms itself closes, seems to me to be eminently
appropriate to all that I have experienced. All that
is past,—all in the prospect of what is to come—calls
for a long, a joyful, a triumphant *Hallelujah!*"

It was, indeed, a long task, and the Christian world,
with one voice, says it was well done. His Commentaries are adapted to the people. They meet, as they
were designed to meet, the common mind. They are
charged with common sense. They are free from the
processes of critical study, yet they furnish ample
proof of it in its results. They are eminently spiritual
and practical. With faithful exposition of the letter
of the word is woven a happy discerning of the mind
of the Spirit. They bear abundant witness to that
true communion with God which their author
testified, if he ever had it in his life, was closely
connected with those calm and quiet morning hours
when his mind was brought into close contact with
the truth inspired by the Holy Ghost. They are
pervaded by those qualities, and they possess those
characteristics, which make them the best—as they
are deservedly the most widely appreciated and most
generally used — Scriptural expositions in any language for the ordinary reader.

Upon the *ministry* of this servant of Jesus, God set early and abundant seal. His favour among the people of his first charge was assured from the outset. He at once made a strong impression on the congregation as a forcible and faithful preacher. His fidelity to his convictions commanded the respect of all. His clear Scriptural expositions, his gentle, yet candid, firm, and fearless applications, his bold assaults upon established iniquities, did not alienate from him the hearts of men, but led them, by the convincing and persuasive power of the Holy Ghost, to give their hearts to God.

A revival of remarkable extent and power occurred during his ministry at Morristown. The windows of heaven were opened over that place, and all the region round about was refreshed with the copious shower. "Mightily grew the Word of God and prevailed." "The name of the Lord Jesus was magnified." Hundreds, it is said, were added to the Church as the result of that glorious work. In the midst of this revival, Mr. Barnes preached a sermon (February 8, 1829) entitled "The Way of Salvation," which was afterwards printed.* It occasioned the sending of a committee from this Church to Morristown, with a view of tendering the author a call to the pastorate of the First Church, if the committee should be favourably impressed. The call was made.

---

* This Sermon appears to have been the germ of a series of Essays, published in one volume under the above title.

Mr. Barnes, in a letter (dated March 25, 1830) to a friend in this city, thus exhibits the spirit with which it was received: "It is very possible that I shall deem it my duty, in consequence of a very surprising and extraordinary event, which has both amazed and over-whelmed me, and the design of Providence in which I cannot understand, to visit your city in a short time."

He accepted this call, and was duly installed as pastor of this church the same year. He found a united people. During the six years of conflict that followed, they "never swerved or hesitated." There can be no better, no prouder testimonial of his people's fidelity than that which is given in his own words. At the age of three-score, reviewing the past, he said: "In every new phase of the now almost forgotten struggle before the Presbytery, the Synod, and the Church at large, the entire congregation stood by me until the great result was reached which gave us peace. None were drawn away; none among us attempted to make a division."*

Into the details of that long and bitter controversy it is not in consonance with my own feelings, it is not in keeping with the spirit of this occasion, it is not in accordance with the known wishes of the sainted dead, that I should enter. They were painful years to Albert Barnes. But through them all he bore himself with a firmness that never passed, by its excess, to obstinacy; with a gentleness, that never

* 'Life at Threescore,' p. 27.

degenerated into weakness; and with a patience, that was never ruffled. Tenaciously holding to what he believed to be the truth; expressing with no "bated breath" his own convictions; submitting "for the sake of order" to what he believed to be an unrighteous decision; acquitted at last by the highest judicatory known in our church; he came out of the conflict as he had entered it—with a character untarnished, and a name above suspicion or reproach. However men may have differed as to the soundness of some of his doctrinal statements and positions, they did not differ as to the purity of his motives and the guilelessness of his spirit. Spectators of the strife, and even participants in it, tell me they never shall forget the Christ-like mien of the man "who took victory with a modesty as great as the patience with which he suffered reproach."

After peace came, he went steadily on with his ministerial work. His pulpit and pastoral ministrations were blessed of God to the conversion of hundreds, and sanctified to the spiritual edification of other hundreds. Frequent revivals have marked the history of his long pastorate. He believed in revivals. In the winter of 1841 he preached a series of sermons on "Revivals of Religion in cities and large towns," their vindication, their influence, their importance, their desirableness, their hindrances, and the duties of Christians in regard to them. These were afterwards published in "The National Preacher."

Chancing to suggest to him, shortly before his decease, the desirableness of a series of articles on this subject, that should appear in some one of our religious papers, and the propriety of their preparation by him, he adopted the suggestion, and assured me he would carry it out. But before he could execute his purpose, he was called to the Church where no revivals are needed.

While thus, however, an advocate of revivals of religion, as warranted in reason and in Scripture, it was not at the expense of doctrinal truth that he favoured them. In the midst of these seasons of special interest he was accustomed to give full exhibition of God's plan of saving men according to His sovereign will and pleasure. And throughout his ministry he grounded his people in the faith by very frequent and full but temperate discussions of the leading doctrines of the Divine Word. Somewhat late in life he said, "I have aimed in my ministry to declare the whole counsel of God. I have embraced the Trinitarian system of religion and the Calvinistic system, and have not concealed the features of these systems from the world. I have endeavoured to set forth the doctrines of human depravity and of the atonement, and of the necessity of regeneration by the Holy Ghost. I have defended the doctrine of decrees, of election, of justification by faith, and of future retribution. I have endeavoured to show to men that they could be saved by no merit of their own, and that their own works will avail them nothing in the matter of justification before God."* Surely he not only "fought a good fight," but he "kept the faith."

At last, by reason of his diminishing power of vision, threatening total blindness if he were not freed from pulpit and pastoral responsibility, he felt called upon to resign, finally and absolutely, his ministerial charge. At his own urgent request, his official relation to this congregation was severed November 18th, 1867, and thereafter his connection was nominal and honorary, though invisible withs of the most tender and most grateful affection bind him still and will for ever, to the hearts of his people. He communicated his wish to the congregation "with deep and painful emotion." He testified that in his long association of thirty-seven years with the session of the church an unkind word had never been spoken, while he had always been welcomed to the homes of the people, and treated by them with unvarying kindness, courtesy, and respect.

After his resignation he continued to the close of his life occasionally ministering to his dear old flock. He was scarcely ever absent from the celebration of the Lord's Supper, and invariably took part in its administration when present. No one who was present will ever forget the last memorial feast we enjoyed together. It seems now as if the coming

* 'Life at Threescore,' p. 28.

K

event cast its shadow there. And yet it was not a shadow; for while our hearts were full to weeping as we sat at the table, and heard that father in Israel allude to the possibility of his never breaking bread with us again, the place seemed like an outer court of Heaven.

On the morning of the last Sabbath of his life, he preached in this pulpit. He unfolded the antagonisms of justice and mercy, the difficulties of their reconciliation, and clearly and fully demonstrated how the difficulties were met and removed in the plan of salvation as revealed in the Word of God. The sermon was extemporaneous—as were all the pulpit efforts of the later years of his life—but it was able and thorough in its presentation of the great theme, and delivered with unwonted animation and vigour. His physical vitality was remarkable, and seemed to be retained to the very hour of his death. The last words I think he ever spoke in this pulpit, were in reply to a remark of mine concerning the sermon he had just delivered. I said to him, "I thank you, Mr. Barnes, for this full, faithful, lucid exposition of God's plan of saving men through the meeting together of justice and mercy in Christ Jesus." "It's about all I know," was his modest and Christian answer. It was but another way of saying what he had said in his sermon at three-score: "Christ Jesus came into the world to save sinners. . . . This is my faith. This is my hope.

I have no other. I desire no other."* Parting with
him that last Sabbath, I expressed our indebtedness
for his service. In the overflow and exuberance of
his bounding health he playfully replied: "When I
get a new charge you may pay me back."

He loved life. It was a joy to him to live. "The
idea of life as such, the desirableness of living,"
seemed to lift and enlarge itself in his mind as he
grew on. It was not that he feared death. But he
shrank from the ordinary accompaniments of death,
from decrepitude, dotage, decay, darkness, the shadow
of death, and the grave. It was not that he feared
what follows death; for he was personally hopeful
in regard to the future world. And his hope was
found alone, as he solemnly said, "in the blood of
Jesus Christ, which cleanseth from all sin." In
the light of that hope, as it brightened in the
advancing years, "the objects of eternity became
overpoweringly bright and grand." And with his
views of heaven he publicly declared that he could
not envy, even if envy were ever proper, one who
was to remain on earth.*

But he loved life as the scene of the development
of the great plans of God. Of all old men I ever
knew, or of whom I ever heard, he cherished the
cheerfullest views of life; of the world; of the certain
progress of the race; of the destiny of man. "Never,"
said he, in his seventieth year, "never in the history

* 'Life at Threescore,' p. 59.

of the world did young men enter on their career with so much to cheer them, to animate them, to inspire them with hope, to call forth their highest powers for the promotion of the great objects which enter into the civilization, the progress, and the happiness of man. The opinions of a man at seventy years of age have been long maturing, and he is not likely materially to change them. I shall cherish these views till I die, and I shall close my eyes in death with bright and glorious hopes in regard to my native land, to the Church, and to the world."

What shall we say of such a man ? What analysis shall we make of his character ? What eulogy shall we pass upon his life ? How did it come about that he rose from comparative obscurity to such a peerless place ? By what methods and appliances did he reach his proud eminence as an author, "an epistle of commendation to the Evangelical churches," an ambassador, and a man ?

First of all, let it be said, as it would be said by him if he could speak to-day, if praise is due any-where, it is not so much to the man, as to the God and Saviour of the man, by whose overruling and guiding Providence Albert Barnes was "called to the king-dom" for such a time and such a work as this; within whose comprehensive plan this life-plan was given its place and successful execution; and who has thus furnished another signal illustration that the steps of a good man are ordered by the Lord.

But while this is true, it is also true that with "our ends" our "rough-hewing" has something to do, as well as God's "shaping." Life, in its issues, is determined by the uses and abuses of a free will. Achievements, under God, are according to qualities of character. Given certain characteristics and endowments, with certain conditions, and we may count on certain results. What Mr. Barnes was accounts for what he did.

One of the marked features of his character was his *rare balance*. He was mentally well-poised. There were no brilliant and transcendent gifts of mind, eclipsing other gifts. There were no faculties that came pre-eminently to the lead, and compelled the following of the rest. He did not excel in the realm of the imagination. He was not tempted to an excess of reasoning by a dominance of the logical faculty. There was no singular and unusual conspicuity given to any power. He was "rounded out" as to his intellectual structure. He never startled, therefore. He never came with the sudden sweep of so-called genius. He was calm, self-poised, even, in all his mental movements; never thrown from equilibrium; never unbalanced.

Along with this was a *rare command* of his faculties. He had them at his beck. They played him no tricks. He could always rely upon them. He could suffer, and still think. He had moods, but they never affected the play of his mental machinery.

There, in that quiet study, when the clock struck the morning hour which he had fixed as the limit of his expository work, he instantly laid down his pen, sometimes in the midst of a paragraph, sometimes in the midst of a sentence, and the next morning he could go on with the thought as well as when he left it. His failing eye-sight involved the necessity of a change in his manner of preaching from the written to the extemporaneous discourse— a change never satisfactory to himself. But his people heard him with as great pleasure as ever. Many avowed that they never liked him so well. He was fitted for an extemporizer; his habits of mind were fixed; he had all his powers well in hand; he could trust to them; and to the very close of his life he went through elaborate, closely-reasoned, thoroughly-wrought-out but unwritten discourses without a trip or a halt, and with an apparent ease that was marvellous. Of course he carefully prepared his train of thought, and commonly with brief notes. But after he had once completed the process, he laid his work upon its mental shelf and left it there. He never thought of it again until he entered the pulpit. While at home on the morning of the Sabbath, after his preparation was made, and while on his way to church, he could be occupied with anything. He gave his theme no thought, and it gave him no thought. When he had occasion to use it he took it down from its shelf, not verbally constructed in his mind and memorized, but *mastered*. And then he preached just what he had designed to preach—sometimes more, but always that. The talent of using his talent, using it to the *full*—he had that, and to a degree rarely equalled.

Add to these characteristics two others—*industry* and *method*—and I think we have the secret of his success in crowding into one life so vast a work for God and humanity. Whatever success he had obtained he himself attributed, under God, to industry. It was to him an abiding source of enjoyment. Habits of industry were begun in early life, and were commended to him by the example of a venerated father. He testified that there were no natural endowments—and that certainly he had none—which could supply their place. For more than thirty years he plodded on in that path of quiet, earnest toil during the early hours of every morning. Through cold and heat, storm and calm, he resorted regularly to his study and persevered in his purpose, leaving the self-imposed task each day only to take up the immediate preparation for his pulpit. From that pulpit he was less frequently absent than is even regarded as justifiable by a faithful ministry, while to his pulpit duties and his pastoral duties he gave an amount of time and labour equal to, if not beyond, the average given by other men in the ministerial calling. Through all the thirty-seven years of his pastorate here, with the exception of the

valuable assistance rendered him in the services of
Rev. Mr. Dickinson and Rev. Mr. Leeds, he was able
for the most part to perform the entire work involved
in his responsible charge without aid, while still
continuing to labour upon his Commentaries.

His industry was coupled with *method*, and this
enhanced greatly the amount and the value of his
work. He had his tasks laid out in systematic order.
He had his "times and seasons" for every purpose.
Order was his first law, of which that resolve never
to pass nine o'clock with his Commentary work, is
characteristic proof. Method appeared in all his
sermons. Method appeared in all his engagements.
Method appeared in all his life. If he once committed himself to an appointment, men came to
know he would be there to meet it. He made,
therefore, the most of his hours. He lost no time.
He moved like clock-work, and hence his movements
told. Every stroke had its place, and went toward
the furtherance of some predetermined plan. As a
rule he kept his appointments to the minute. He often
waited for others. They seldom waited for him.

He had no capital when he began life. He had no
powerful patronage to assist him. He had no one
brilliant natural endowment conspicuous above the
rest. Balance of faculties, and command of faculties,
industry and method; and behold the life-work !
What an example for young men! What an example
for those now entering the ministry !

But I hasten to speak of his other and moral qualities. His character was marked by a *rigid conscientiousness.* He would do no wrong if he knew it. What he conceived to be duty must be done, if the power could be commanded to do it. Sometimes, and to some judgments, his inflexible adherence to a conviction might have assumed the form and appearance of a scrupulosity. But Albert Barnes would sooner die than violate his conscience. He opposed, in common with a large body of the Christian people of this city, the introduction of the running of street-cars on the Sabbath, on principle. The opposition proved useless. But though the use of the cars would have greatly convenienced him, he never rode in them on the Sabbath, for that (in his judgment) would have placed the principle under his feet.

With a rigid conscientiousness, we commonly associate hardness and harshness, severity and sternness of judgment; the elements that go to make up the *persecutor* are frequently attached to this quality. Some of the cruellest and most heartless deeds known to history have been honestly done in the name of conscience. Saul of Tarsus verily thought he was doing God service in hating the so-called "vile Christian dogs," and persecuting them to the death. But the spirit of persecution never had a home in this generous man's breast. His heart was too full of heaven-born charities, and his conscientiousness was balanced too well by gentle and loving tenderness for that. Though persecuted himself, he never persecuted another. His conscientiousness never could have impelled him to embitter any life by an active and envenomed opposition.

Yet he was *firm*. No one was truer to truth than he. Guiltless of all deceit, and guileless, he "*spoke the truth in his heart.*" He held to it as he held to his hope of eternal life—to every minutest shade of it, as it presented itself to his mind. Nothing could ever sweep him from these moorings. He accepted truth with caution. His naturally sceptical mind led him to examine with carefulness and utmost candour whatever addressed itself to his understanding. But when once accepted, he rested in it as men do in that where lie their dearest hopes. He stood then, as if with a foundation like the everlasting hills. Men might reason, passions might rage, storms might burst, but these could never break this brave spirit's hold of what he deemed to be the truth.

But time fails me even to hint at the variety of his excellences,—his gentlemanliness, his affectionate- ness, his humility, his childlikeness, his love of home, his rare courtesy; while through all and over all, giving a beauty and harmony and glory to all, was his *piety*, born wholly of the grace of God. He walked among men as one who walked with God. They took knowledge of him that he had been with Jesus. And this life lifted him to a higher sphere than that of mere office and authorship. It adorned him with a simplicity and a dignity that no achievement of learning and no royalty of wisdom could win and wear. It transformed his Christ-like spirit more and more until it seemed as if he stood bathed in the glory beaming down upon him from the eternal throne, and as if almost from this side of the river he looked into the other country " beholding the King in His beauty " and " seeing Him as He is." It brought him to the close of his earthly life like a shock of corn fully ripe.

At last God heard his prayer, that *" some disease not tardy to perform its destined office, yet with gentle stroke,"* might dismiss him to a safe retreat. The path which reaches heaven glowed with the steps of the angels as they swept earthward to bear him home. The stroke was gentle. He did not know when it touched him. He fell asleep and woke with God !

" No chariot of fire, no coursers of flame
    Were needed to bear thee away to thy rest ;
  The Lord of the Mansions just whispered thy name,
    And drew thy head gently to sleep on His breast.

  Mortality's raiment laid softly aside ;
    No valley of death, and no river to pass ;
  In an instant, the doors of the casket flew wide,
    And the spirit was gone, like a breath on the glass.

The bondsman's defender, unwearied and strong,
    Ever preaching the freedom Christ bought with His Cross;
Unyielding to aught that bore semblance of wrong,
    Counting honours, and talents, and gold as but dross.

So honest, that doubt never breathed on thy fame;
    So truthful, suspicion grew mute at thy word;
Beloved disciple! revering the name,
    And following so closely the steps of thy Lord.

As humble and child-like as childhood itself;
    As wise as the serpent, as pure as the dove;
As dust in the balance were profit or wealth,
    Compared with the Gospel of Christ and His Love.

'Twas fitting that death should be swift as a flash;
    Life bore a long record unceasingly bright;
No swerving from duty, no passions to clash
    With the glory of God, and the cause of the right.

Like Enoch of old, thou hast passed to the skies,—
    An instant wert here—an instant wert gone;
And we waiting outside, with tears in our eyes,
    And thou in the glory that circles the Throne."

THE END.

LONDON: KNIGHT, PRINTER, BARTHOLOMEW CLOSE.

[*Note.*—A few copies of *Life at Threescore*, by ALBERT BARNES, referred to in the preceding Memorial Sermon, still remain on sale. A copy will be sent free by Post on receipt of Six Postage Stamps, addressed, Mr. EDWARD KNIGHT, Printer, Bartholomew Close, London, E.C.]

ALBERT BARNES AS A COMMENTATOR.

From the American Biblical Repository.

"Mr. Barnes's style is plain, simple, and direct; and though his pages teem with the *material* of deep scholarship, yet he is, for the most part, eminently happy in making himself intelligible and interesting to every class; while the rich practical remarks, every now and then grafted upon the critical details, transfuse the devotional spirit of the writer into the bosom of his reader."

From the Rev. N. McMichael, Prof. of Eccles. U. P. Synod.

"Barnes has many excellences as a commentator. His industry is great, and he has made a free but not unfair use of all available sources of information. Possessed naturally of a clear and vigorous understanding, his opinions are uniformly expressed in a brief, perspicuous manner. He has a singular facility in drawing practical conclusions from the doctrinal statements and historical incidents of the Scripture. They are distinguished by good sense and piety; they are natural without being obvious; and often so striking and pointed as to partake of the character of originality."

From the Rev. William Brock, Bloomsbury, London.

"Barnes is so well known in this country as a commentator who combines some of the most important qualifications for the work he has undertaken, that he needs no further recommendation. I know no guide to the understanding of the sacred oracles more trustworthy. With respectable biblical scholarship, there is connected so much of evangelical sentiment, and genuine spirituality of mind, that I earnestly wish the work were in the hands of all persons who are engaged as missionaries or teachers of the young."

From the Rev. H. Cooke, D.D., LL.D., Belfast.

"His style is generally plain and perspicuous, but where occasion offers, energetic and effective."

From the Rev. John Harris, D.D., Author of "Mammon."

"Barnes is an admirable commentator. The ease and vigour of his style; the clear and natural manner in which he elicits the sense of the text; the point, variety, and impressiveness of his practical reflections, and the evangelical spirit which pervades the whole, combine to render him deservedly popular."

I

NOTES ON THE PSALMS.

By ALBERT BARNES.

Complete in Three Volumes, 12s. (4s. each), cloth, uniform with
"COBBIN'S" and "CUMMING'S" Editions.

[The Volumes to match *Cobbin's* Edition may be had in the new style of
binding, as now issued by Gall and Inglis ; and also in the *Brown* cloth,
embossed, as formerly published. In ordering, it is essential to say which
Edition and style of binding is required.]

From late Rev. W. B. MACKENZIE, M.A., *Vicar of St. James', Holloway.*

"Mr. Barnes's Commentary on the Psalms, here carefully edited, and
admirably got up by his English publisher, possesses the same excellences
which have gained so wide a reputation and unquestioned usefulness for
his other works. Sufficiently critical to elucidate the meaning of the
Psalmist, this exposition excels in its practical bearing upon the duties and
vicissitudes of a religious life. It is not the production of a learned recluse
shut out from the conflicts of the outer world, but of a servant of Christ long
inured to the trials of faith, who felt himself strengthened and refreshed by
those precious Scripture portions here prepared anew for the edification of
others. He presents it to the world as his last literary production. Other
portions of his valuable works, written before his Commentary on the Psalms,
may yet, it is hoped, be published ;—in fact, a Life of St. Paul from Mr.
Barnes's pen, in the course of publication, now lies before us, which will add
to the riches of our practical theology, already owing no small debt of gratitude to this able and indefatigable writer."

From the Rev. HENRY ALLON, *Islington.*

"I have looked through Mr. Barnes' volumes on the Psalms with interest,
and am inclined to think that his treatment of the Book of Psalms is more
valuable and successful than any of his previous expositions,—probably in
virtue of a natural law. The Book of Psalms is in feeling and expression
the most spiritual of all the books of Scripture ; and it is natural that a
writer coming to it, as Mr. Barnes does, in the maturity of Christian experience and the ripeness of Christian feeling, and with the tenderness of
incipient physical infirmity upon him, should largely identify it with his own
feelings. The volumes have critically all the qualities if not of the highest
scholarship, yet of careful and wide reading, robust common sense, and
practical spiritual aim, which have made Mr. Barnes' Commentaries much
more valuable than works of greater pretension and learning. There is,
too, a freedom and breadth about his treatment of the imprecatory Psalms,
for instance, which is not always to be found in advanced years. Mr.
Barnes combines the utmost reverence with a scholarly fidelity to fact and
construction. We want nothing more in these days than a fearless accept-
ance of the Sacred Text, so as to induce a resolute rejection of all pre-
conceived theories as to what it *ought* to mean. Mr. Barnes owes very
much to his English Editor, whose scholarship and patient care are beyond
all praise,"

2

Barnes's Notes on the Psalms.

From the Rev. FRANCIS TUCKER, *Camden Road Chapel.*

" In his Commentary on the Psalms, Mr. Barnes keeps up the reputation he has gained so widely. There is the same fulness, the same fairness, and the same attachment to evangelic truth. The multitudes of his admirers will be glad to secure these attractive-looking volumes." .

" Mr. Barnes has brought to his work a considerable amount of well-digested material, and a matured Christian character. A very competent scholarship is evident, though it is not cumbrous, and does not bristle forbiddingly in his pages. An excellent analysis is given of every Psalm, in which the authorship, the occasion on which it was written, and its contents are summarily presented. . . . The exposition is good, and is accompanied by appropriate reflections, which will prove of value to general readers."—*Wesleyan-Methodist Magazine.*

" We owe much to Mr. Barnes, and these volumes show us at what toil, what expense of life and labour, it has been prosecuted. . . . We should be glad, were it possible, to give some further specimens of the easy and happy style of Mr. Barnes as a commentator ; we might style it unrivalled, but such eulogies are easily scattered abroad, and have no real value attached to them."—*Christian Observer.*

" It is no small merit that Mr. Barnes has produced what, in our view, is the best Commentary for general use which has yet appeared upon the Book of Psalms. His reputation as a commentator, the great need for such a work, and the manifold excellences of this exposition, will secure for these volumes a wide and rapid sale."—*Methodist Recorder.*

" The name of Albert Barnes is a household name on both sides of the Atlantic, and it is respected and beloved wherever known. . . . For twelve long years he has devoted himself to preparing his Commentary on the Book of Psalms ; and we are mistaken if this his last work will not be reckoned among the best, if not the best book which has proceeded from his pen."—*Glasgow Christian News.*

" A valuable acquisition to our theological literature."—*Methodist New Connexion Magazine.*

" The Notes on the Psalms have the peculiar charm belonging to all the writings of this devout and able Commentator, and they need no recommendation."—*Literary World.*

" Ably written, replete with scholarly ability, and a graceful tribute to our Biblical literature."—*Preston Chronicle.*

" Barnes approaches his subject with common sense as well as scholarship, and does his work as if he meant people to profit by it."—*Hastings News.*

" It bears all the marks of that careful study and exercise of sound judgment which so distinguish his former works."—*South Bucks Free Press.*

" The Notes on the Psalms may be considered the very choicest of the Author's works."—*Shields Daily News.*

" It has all the excellences of his Notes upon the Epistles, as well as those upon Job, Isaiah, and Daniel."—*Reformed Presbyterian Magazine.*

" Albert Barnes has obtained a very high position as a popular and exceedingly useful Commentator."—*Banner of Ulster.*

" Those who have read Mr. Barnes's other works will know what to expect, and will not be disappointed."—*Portadown News.*

" We have studied some of the Psalms through the medium of Mr. Barnes's Notes, and we have always been instructed and refreshed. He who reads the Psalms for devotional purposes, as well as he who studies them that he may speak to others words of comfort and strength, will find Mr. Barnes a good companion and fellow-helper."—*Pulpit Analyst.*

London : Hamilton & Co. ; George Routledge & Sons.
Edinburgh : Gall & Inglis (for " Cobbin's Edition").

New Edition, 474 pages, 3s. 6d. cloth ; extra cloth, bevelled, 4s. 6d.

THE WAY OF SALVATION,

ILLUSTRATED AND EXPLAINED.

By ALBERT BARNES.

" In its general arrangement, the volume begins with a consideration of the claims of the Bible as a guide on the subject of religion
(Section I.), and with an effort to show (Section II.) that the
acknowledged obscurities in that book should not deter us from
accrediting its claims ; with a statement (Section III.) of the claims
of Christianity, and an attempt to show (Section IV.) that the condition of man could not be benefited by the rejection of Christianity,
and that the same difficulties precisely would remain, with no known
method whatever of relief.   The next object (Section V.) is to show
that Christianity reveals the true ground of the importance attributed
to man in the plan of salvation ; that the earth is fitted to be a place
of probation (Section VI.), and that man is actually on probation
(Section VII.) ; and that in religion, as in other things, he should
accommodate himself to what are the actual arrangements of the
Divine government (Section VIII.)   The next object is to explain
the condition in which the Gospel FINDS man—as an actual state
which Christianity did not originate, for which it is not responsible,
and which is a simple *matter of fact* in which all men are equally
interested, whatever system of religion may be true or false (Section
IX.) ; a state which naturally prompts to the inquiry what must be
done in order to be saved—an inquiry which springs up in the heart
of man everywhere, and in reference to which man pants for an
answer (Section X.)   This is followed (Sections XI.—XIV.) by a
description of the struggles of a convicted sinner—and by an attempt
to show what is *necessary*, in the nature of things, to give peace to
a mind in that condition.   To meet the case, the mind thus anxious
is directed to the mercy of God (Section XV.), and the effort is
made to show that it is only an atonement for sin that can give
permanent peace to the soul conscious of guilt (Section XVI., XVII.)
The doctrine of Regeneration, or the new birth, is then considered
(Section XVIII.—XX.) ; an attempt is made to vindicate and explain
the *conditions*—repentance and faith—which are made necessary to
salvation, and to show not only their place in a revealed system of
religion, but their relation to the human mind and the circumstances
in which man is placed (Sections XXI.—XXVIII.) ; and the whole
series is closed (Sections XXIX.—XXXVI.) by a consideration of the
nature of justification, or the method by which a sinner may be just
with God.   It will be seen that these topics embrace the most
material and important inquiries which come before the mind on the
question *how man may be saved* ; and if a correct representation is
given of them, they will furnish to an inquirer after truth a just view
of the way of salvation.

" I commit this volume to the public with the hope that it may

6

be found to be a safe guide on the most momentous inquiry which can come before the human mind. I have abundant occasion for gratitude for the manner in which the volumes that I have published heretofore have been received by the British public, as well as by my own countrymen ; as I would hope that this volume may contribute something to the diffusion of the knowledge of the great principles of religious duty and doctrine which has been the labour of my life to illustrate and defend."—*ALBERT BARNES.*

Essays on Science and Theology.

By ALBERT BARNES. Crown 8vo., 376 pp., 3s. 6d. cloth.

CONTENTS :—1. Progress and Tendency of Science. 2. Literature and Science of America. 3. Position of the Christian Scholar. 4. Desire of Reputation. 5. Choice of Profession. 6. The Christian Ministry. 7. Thoughts on Theology. 8. Review of Butler's Analogy. 9. The Law of Paradise. 10. Relation of Theology to Preaching. 11. Preaching to the Conscience. 12. Practical Preaching.

"The Author has given his cordial sanction to the publishing of this Edition, and has expressed his approbation of the selection and general arrangement of the Essays in their present form. In preparing them for the English public, I have considered it advisable to transpose them, as it appeared that, by an alteration in their sequence, a unity of design might be preserved which would render the work more attractive and profitable as a whole. By such arrangement, the Author's views are first given as to the historic progress and actual condition of literature and science, particularly in his own country, as well as the bearing which these have upon the interests of religion. After these general remarks, the reader's attention is called to the Desire of Reputation, which is so powerful a motive and so active an auxiliary to the pursuit of knowledge. The Choice of a Profession naturally presents itself as the next theme of consideration ; and this Essay I would especially recommend for the forcible and practical remarks which are embodied in it. For such as have chosen the ministerial profession, the next section will have peculiar interest. The four following Essays are replete with most valuable remarks on various theological points connected with the defence and integrity of the faith ; and those at the conclusion are mainly designed to set forth the kind of preaching which is most needed to meet the wants of the present age, and to subserve the great end of the gospel-ministry in the winning of immortal souls."

LONDON : HAMILTON, ADAMS, & CO., 32, Paternoster Row.

Second Edition, Crown 8vo, with Illustrations, 3s. 6d. cloth.

NIGHT UNTO NIGHT:

A Selection of Bible Scenes.

By REV. DANIEL MARCH, D.D.

Part I.—1. The Teachings of Night. 2. The Last Night of Sodom. 3. Abraham's Night Vision at Beersheba. 4. Jacob's Night at Bethel. 5. Jacob's Night of Wrestling. 6. The Last Night of Israel in Egypt. 7. The Night Passage of the Sea. 8. Saul's Night at Endor. 9. David's Night at the Jordan. 10. Elijah's Night in the Desert. 11. Jonah's Night at Nineveh. 12. The Night Watch on Mount Seir. 13. The Night of Tears. 14. The Night Feast of Belshazzar.

Part II.—1. A Night with Jesus at Jerusalem. 2. A Night of Prayer on the Mountain. 3. Night Storm on the Sea. 4. The Night of Peter's Temptation. 5. The Night of Agony in Gethsemane. 6. The First Night after the Resurrection. 7. The Night of Fruitless Toil. 8. Angel Visits in the Night. 9. Midnight in the Prison at Philippi. 10. Paul's Night on the Deep. 11. No Night in Heaven.

"Certain well-known Night Scenes of Scripture are here sketched with a vividness and graphic force which make us spectators of the varied incidents; while the lessons that are drawn from them of warning, of hope, or of duty, are brought home to the heart and conscience with tenderness and power."—*British Quarterly Review.*

"Dr. March has vividly conceived and very graphically described many Bible scenes which were associated with the night, both in the Old and New Testaments. The fact of Dr. March's personal visit to the lands of the Bible enables him to speak with authority upon many matters. The whole book is suggestive and striking. We have sketches of the Last Night of Sodom, the Last Night of Israel in Egypt, the Night Passage of the Sea, and Saul's Night at Endor, with all the memorable night scenes which are spoken of in the Bible story. We commend the volume to all ministers for examples of a fresh and vivid style in the treatment of such subjects; and with confidence to all other persons who want to read, or to give away, a most interesting book." —*Literary World.*

"The nights of the Bible have a strange amount of doing and suffering connected with them, and it is to the lessons which are to be drawn from these wonderful pieces of nightwork that Dr. March has sought to turn the reader's attention."—*The Rock.*

"Dr. March is already known to numerous English readers as the author of 'Walks and Homes of Jesus.' The present volume is a selection of Night Scenes in Scripture history—they are explained, commented on, and the practical lessons arising from them are well applied. . . 'Night unto Night' is one of the cheapest books we have seen for some time. It is printed and got up in a style which made us question whether there was not some mistake about the price advertised for so elegant a volume."—*Watchman.*

"From some of the Night Scenes in sacred history the author has drawn many profitable lessons for the dark hours of life, and seeks to cheer and guide Christian pilgrims on their way to that land where 'there shall be no night.' The book is divided into two parts—'Scenes from the Old Testament' and 'Scenes from the New Testament,'—and in each of these the most choice selections have been made. The book is graphically and well-written throughout, and the scenes he depicts are truthfully drawn, the author having had opportunities of personally verifying the researches of others in the Holy Land." —*Weekly Review.*

LONDON: HAMILTON, ADAMS, & CO., 32, Paternoster Row.

8

Second Edition, with Illustrations, Crown 8vo., 2s. 6d. cloth.

𝔚𝔞𝔩𝔨𝔰 𝔞𝔫𝔡 𝔥𝔬𝔪𝔢𝔰 𝔬𝔣 𝔍𝔢𝔰𝔲𝔰.

By Rev. DANIEL MARCH, D.D.

A few copies handsomely printed on toned paper, extra cloth gilt, 3s. 6d.

" I regard the ' Walks and Homes of Jesus' as a very interesting and valuable work. The plan is new; the style is very attractive; the reflections are very just; and the whole character of the work such as is fitted to make a good impression . . Dr. March is an eloquent preacher, a fine scholar, and a most excellent man."—Albert Barnes.

" Taking the Gospel record for his guide, and keeping the present aspect of Palestine ever in mind, Dr. March introduces us to Bethlehem, Nazareth, Capernaum, Bethesda, Tabor, Jericho, Bethany, and Jerusalem, and traces the walks of Jesus with men. . . . The descriptive passages are not fancy sketches. The fine imagination of the writer has indeed given life and reality to his descriptions, but truth has not been sacrificed to pictorial effect. The plan on which the book has been formed is, to us, original : the conception good, and the style reminds us of the late Dr. Hamilton."—*Christian World.*

" Dr. March's object, in the ' Walks and Homes of Jesus,' has been to look upon our Lord as He was seen by the men of His time, and to combine with this view the more mature and instructed impressions which spring from faith in His redeeming work and His Divine nature. He is obviously very familiar with the physical aspect of Palestine, and describes, often in a very graphic manner, the different places where our Lord sojourned. . . . Altogether, it is a popular and highly readable presentation of the life of Him to whom we owe every blessing, and whose glory, when seen with the spiritual eye, fills the heart with wonder and the lips with praise."—*Reformed Presbyterian Review.*

" Step by step we are conducted through the vale of humiliation, from Bethlehem to Jerusalem—from the manger to the cross. Our interest is not allowed to flag throughout the journey, and often our hearts are made to burn within us as we walk with Jesus in the way. . . . We can yield a ready and hearty assent to all Dr. March's statements of moral and spiritual truths, to which he has rightly subordinated all besides. The main object which he keeps steadily before him is, ' to set forth the human and historic reality of the Divine Personage,' and in in this he has been eminently successful."—*Weekly Review.*

" Teems with the deepes devotional thought, called up by the contemplation of the scenes of our blessed Lord's ministry."—*The Rock.*

Daily Bible Teachings.

By T. S. Henderson. 2s. cloth; 2s. 6d. extra cloth gilt; 3s. 6d. morocco.

" I have now had time to examine ' Daily Bible Teachings ' pretty thoroughly, and I consider it to be admirably adapted to the purpose for which it was written. The texts are impartially chosen from the whole Bible, and the treatment of them is plain, practical, and in perfectly good taste. No child can fail to be interested by the lively style in which the daily Teachings are given, and by the illustrations and anecdotes with which they are interspersed."

Rev. C. L. Ranken, *Richmond, Surrey.*

London : Hamilton, Adams, & Co., 32, Paternoster Row.

9

Dedicated by permission to the Archbishop of Canterbury.

Fourth Edition, crown 8vo., printed on toned paper, 2s. 6d. cloth.

AGNES AND THE LITTLE KEY;

Or, Bereaved Parents Instructed and Comforted.

WITH A RECOMMENDATORY PREFACE

By MISS MARSH.

" Upon this, the fourth edition of a choice book, we need make no comment, but we may quote a few words from the very beautiful preface, instructive as they are to all believers who desire to minister as "sons of consolation" :—

"It is the tone of simple truth, the *reality* in this record of an earthly sorrow, gradually gilded and finally glorified by a Heavenly Hope and Faith, which renders it peculiarly suitable to mourners. Just enough of the anguish of a wounded heart is expressed to prove that no mere passing pang was inflicted by the loss of the 'desire' of those parents' 'eyes.' And in their efforts 'to comfort them which were in any trouble by the comfort wherewith they themselves were comforted of God,' there is none of that didactic strain of dry, theological consolation, or hard, unsympathising denunciation of all impassioned grief—too frequently the tone assumed in books written for mourners—which has made many a stricken soul exclaim, 'Thou speakest as one who has never lost a son.'"

"Mourners can bear to be comforted when they have been permitted to weep freely. Many well-meant attempts to give comfort, and to make trial teach, fail sadly, because the steps of approach are too rapid, or the voice sounds strange, unappreciating sorrow."

The Record.

"We can well understand how this touching story unfolded in these pathetic pages has become so popular, as to ask for itself a fourth edition, which it has now reached. The few incidents recorded, and the beauty of holiness which graces and glorifies the whole tissue of the story, cannot fail to make pleasant and useful impressions on the reader. The passages of poetry, and of Scripture, introduced for illustrative purposes, are extremely well chosen, and very apt for the purpose."—*Rock.*

"This book is written by a father, who has passed through the great sorrow of losing a beloved child ; and who has found out the secret of imparting to his fellow-mourners 'the comfort wherewith he himself has been comforted.' . . . It is a sweet and holy-hearted book. Its first pages seemed to us over sentimental, perhaps trivial,—but *we*, thank God, have never tasted the bitterness this father has known, and we were not in prepared sympathy with the writer. On reading further, our feelings quite changed ; and we now speak of it with tenderness and admiration."—

Nonconformist.

LONDON : HAMILTON, ADAMS, & CO., 32, Paternoster Row.

12